Snow on the Roof— Fire Inside

Life Lived with Throttle Open Wide

Bob McCluskey

PublishAmerica
Baltimore

ISBN: 978-1-60749-840-7 (softcover)
ISBN: 978-1-4489-9285-0 (hardcover)
PUBLISHED BY PUBLISHAMERICA, LLLP
www.publishamerica.com
Baltimore

Printed in the United States of America

Dedication

After 54 years of marriage to my sweetheart Margaret, her passing in 2008, left a big hole in my life. The last year now, since her passing, has been a difficult transition time in personal terms, as well as a productive time, poetically speaking…Some of the poetry in this book, speaks to these issues. I could not, in good conscience, release this book of poetry without paying tribute to Margaret's leavening influence over my life, and for such a very long time. Without her influence, I have no doubt that my creative juices would have been very dry indeed. And so…Here's to You, Sweetheart…Thanks' a Million, eh!

Table of Contents

MY TESTIMONY

How could I know at the start of my life
That the source of my nurture—my fathers wife
Reflected a facet of Godly love
Poured out from the Father of Lights above
FOR GOD IS LOVE

And then as I grew and the years went by
I made my demands, never wondering why
Moms giving and loving were ever the norm
Never withheld when I didn't perform
FOR GOD IS LOVE

I grew into manhood and revelled in strength
Went away from home and traveled at length
Took love where I found it, with scarcely a thought
Of Gods Love rejected and given for nought
FOR GOD IS LOVE

Then in Gods good time, He brought into my life
His Love through the one who became my wife
Once more I was blessed with nurturing love
Still blind to the source—that it came from above
FOR GOD IS LOVE

As the years rolled by, I continued to take
From my daughters and wife, love I needed to make
Me happy I thought—But an emptiness grew
Unabated by wine or possessions anew
FOR GOD IS LOVE

Till at last with despair, past the middle of life
Wine soaked and empty, no marriage or wife
No resources or hope—I was beaten and sore
But at last God could enter and finally pour
in HIS HEALING LOVE.

What a glorious bursting forth of light
What a transformation to daylight from night
What a renewal—what a delight
Everything lovely and shiny and bright
FOR GOD IS LOVE.

Now that right order's established and set
My love for my family is greater yet
But more than this as I look around
I find love in the family of God to abound
FOR GOD IS LOVE

And I see at the right hand of Christian brothers
Gods gift of love in wives, sisters and mothers
Sustaining and nurturing—giving them life
Reflecting Gods love throughout blessing or strife
FOR GOD IS LOVE

And each son in Gods kingdom's abundantly blessed
By the Love of God through His daughters expressed
Whether single or wed, as they touch our life
We come closer to God through our sisters in Christ
FOR GOD IS LOVE

THE REFRIGERATOR BALL

March, 2008

Sometimes through the night, when all's fast asleep,
something in the kitchen, starts to stir and to creak.

The refrigerator opens, slowly, just a bit,
and you'd start to see movement, by the light that's lit.

The family pup that's sleeping, on the kitchen chair,
woke up feeling foggy, and began to stare.

At the parade of fruit and veggies, and began to growl,
but the watermelon scared him, and he scooted with a howl.

Somehow they knew that nothing, would disturb their shiveree,
'cause the whole world was snoring, at half past three.

There was syncopated movement, as they stood on one spot,
while the rubber band was tuning up, and stretching quite a lot.

When at last, in the rubber band, the elastics notes were true.
they started playing nursery rhymes, that everybody knew.

All the fruit and veggies danced, Oh how their feet flew,
no worry about food groups, they were like a big stew.

So they paired off together, and it really was a sight,
as they danced around the counter top, all through the night.

Mister lettuce with miss tomato, and she blushed deep red,
as twirling through the dancers, all around they sped.

For we know they blend together well, and well they should,
'cause a lettuce and tomato sandwich, tastes real good.

And different kinds of berries, were twirling in a bowl,
for blending all together, was tonight their goal.

I saw mister celery stick, with his leafy top thatch,
waltzing miss cheese whiz, they made a perfect match.

There goes mister broccoli, with prim miss cauliflower,
looking lovely all in white, they danced by the hour.

Here they come, there they go, they put on quite a dancing show,
round and round, in and out, gaily twirling all about.

But now the dawn was breaking, lights turned on up above,
to dance another hour or two, they all would love.

But helter skelter they all rushed, down upon the floor,
to the refrigerator fly, then open up the door.

They jump up and take their place, right where they belong,
they had a lovely time tonight, and danced to every song.

They all were saying their goodbyes, they knew what did await,
With all this hungry household, they'd soon be on a plate.

But don't be sad, they're really glad, they want to meet their fate,
They know why God created them, and this makes them feel great.

So now into the kitchen, with sleep upon their face,
come Mom and Dad for breakfast, finding everything in place.

They never dreamed what happened, as they glance up at the clock,
They'd really get an ear full, if that little dog could talk.

ULTIMATE DESTINATIONS

March, 2009

Will we all walk those streets of gold,
where light will radiate I'm told.
From source eternal, un-electric,
one source only…un-eclectic.

We will meet folks, we didn't know,
some we were certain, wouldn't show.
Some thought this trip, we'd never make,
from shock, they'll do a double take.

If we could be in charge, like God,
our choices, He would not applaud.
Might let some in, who'd not yet died,
while locked out saints, stand mystified.

So now, let's look the other way,
deep into hell, where demons play.
If we determined who would burn,
the Devil'd be un-taciturn.

We'd bar the door, and lock the gate,
the Devil, we could not placate.
Those demon's would be unemployed,
of rebels, hell would be devoid.

So now, where could rebellion go,
turn heaven into hell, we know.
Saints cannot burn, we hear them shout,
so down in hell, the fires go out.

Then wouldn't we create a mess,
great bedlam now, I must confess.
Please Lord, take back authority,
Your perfect way…our ardent plea.

PRIDE GROWETH BEFORE A STALL

March, 2009

While driving in my Lincoln Continental yesterday,
Started sliding on a hidden patch of ice.
When a speeding Austin Healy, tried to take the right of way,
By passing on my right, which wasn't nice.

Now this made me quite indignant, and I know that you'll agree,
This ungentlemanly driving was unsafe.
And the smirk that he was wearing, as he turned to stare at me,
Made me want to wipe that smirk right off his face.

Then I couldn't keep from smiling, when I saw him lose control,
He too never saw the ice, and hit a tree.
Then I knew he was in danger, that his car could start to roll,
But it really served him right, you will agree.

When I left my car to help him, what I found to my chagrin,
Was my Pastor quite bewildered in his seat.
He really wasn't speeding, 'twas the ice that made him spin,
That he managed to avoid me…quite a feat.

And the smirk I saw him wearing…really not a smirk at all,
'twas a look of raw unmitigated fear.
And the thing he was afraid of, was that he might do me harm,
By driving at full speed into my rear.

Then my attitude, from shame, did a very quick u-turn,
My relationship with God, I must renew.
I'm very happy to report, his car's ok, I was to learn,
And I followed him back home…the thing to do.

I must admit that my contrition, caused a change in how I live,
Next Sunday when collection plate came by.
If I didn't make an increase, to the pittance that I give,
Then I nevermore could look him in the eye.

And the lesson that I learned, and maybe this could help us all,
Is, that things in life…not always what they seem.
If I start to get too haughty, pride can go before a fall,
With repentance, all that's lost, God can redeem.

WW2, WHAT DID I DO?

March, 2009

Nineteen forty three, war all over the world, I'm a seventeen year old
lad,
Wet behind the ear, no conception of fear, wanting some action bad.
The R.C.A.F. was looking for boys, to be Wireless Air Gunner's,
brave.
I paid them a visit, they invited me in, and asked if I'd started to
shave.

Then after they had their little joke, we got down to business for
real,
Took a few of us into another room, and ordered us all to peel.
Down to the buff, and if that's not enough, we had to bend over and
cough,
They checked places we never knew we had, then put on the clothes
we took off.

Then off to the barber we marched enmass, trying hard not to fall out
of step,
He was not a hair stylist, I hasten to add, but at scalping he showed
lots of pep.
Then into another building we marched, where they started throwing
us clothes,
How they're able to size us up at a glance, heaven only knows.

In the Horse Palace at the C.N.E., a nice Sergeant would billet us
next,
Two attractive cots in each horses stall, we were all feeling quite
perplexed.
But after a week in that dampness and cold, I started to feel quite
sick,
To Chorley Park Military Hospital, they transferred me pretty quick.

Bronchial Asthma, I was diagnosed, a hospital stay…what a pain,
All my new found friends in the R.C.A.F., I never would see again.
I soon was well, but it's chronic, and weak eyes, so they threw me
out,
Back on civvy street, this hero's returned, so now I'm casting about.

Rejected by the Air force, I hitch-hiked to Montreal,
To try the Merchant Navy, I went to the Hiring Hall,
Rejection again, no experience, so I couldn't go to sea,
But they'd hire me on the Lake Boats, a Trimmer I would be.

I signed on to the William Schupp, a Canaler, ten thousand tons,
A coal burner, two boilers, four fires for steam, that's the way she
runs.
Four hours on, four hours off, each day around the clock,
Fireman would clean two fires a shift, keep up steam, however she'd
rock.

I picked her up at the Welland Canal, and now I'm adventure bound,
At the end of the season, through terrible storm, we'd lay up in
Owen Sound.
We'd haul coal from Quebec to Thunder Bay, though we're only a
little ship,
Bring back wheat through the Welland Canal, where we're small
enough to fit.

We'd coal up at Sandusky, Ohio, on the American side,
We're on the way, to Thunder Bay…in the fire-hold, stripped to the
hide.
I'm the trimmer, we start pulling fires, one under each boiler…each
watch,
The Fireman pulls hot coals on the deck, takes a swig from a Mickey
of Scotch.

My job's to pour buckets of water, on the coals, so he's able to toil,
Over hot clinkers, the fire rebuild, so the steam will continue to boil.
I shovel ashes into the ash-guns, and they're pumped out over the
side.
In the storm later on, with no covers, those two holes were open
wide.

The storm that I'm referring to, was December, nineteen forty four,
Gale force winds and record snow, Ontario suffered sore.
In Toronto, people skied to work, a street car was blown on it's side,
On lake Superior, sailing for home, our ship almost turned on it's side.

With our hearts in our mouths, she righted herself, rolling with the
next wave,
On her beams end, bow up in the sky, she'll be finished, if hatches
cave.
As she shudders and shakes…fights for her life, waves break over
the ship,
Ice continues to build, if top heavy she gets, this could easily cause
her to flip.

While down in the fire-hold, stripped to the waist, it looked like a
scene from hell,
From those sizzling clinkers, clouds of steam…bad trouble if
pressure fell.
Lake water pours out on the fire-hold floor, from those open holes
on the side,
Soaking the coal that we have to use, causing steam pressure to
slide.

Vague figures obscured by steamy mist, as we toil to keep pressure up,
For if headway we lose…sideways we'll turn…the end of the
William Schupp.
At the end of our watch, we have to climb up, to the after-house,
with fear,
Not out on the deck, we'd be swept away, we can judge the waves
from up here.

With the roll of the ship, the starboard submerged…port side cabin
door was dry,

Then you'd drop to the deck, race around to the door, you had to be
pretty spry.
They'd unlock from within, to let you in, but one time they were too
slow,
The ship rolled back again, had a grip of pain, held my breath,
'cause under I go.

But it worked out alright, you can tell I survived, as we slowly
headed for port,
That guy finished his Mickey, I'm sure when we dock, he'll find
himself a quart.
As we swaggered ashore, people stared with awe, at the ice built up
on our ship,
But we acted as if it was nothing at all…not to worry…just part of
the trip.

LIFE'S PATHWAY/SOLILOQUY

March, 2009

MORN...BORN

WHO...YOU

MOM'S, BREAST

FOOD...BEST

GROW...KNOW

RAIN...SNOW

GAME...PLAY

ALL...DAY

SUN...FUN

DARK...RUN

BOY...JOY

NEW...TOY

LIFE...NEW

ME...YOU

GIRL...CURL

MISS...KISS

RING...CLING

WED...BLISS

WIFE...STRIFE

WILD...CHILD

WAR...SCORE

WHAT...FOR

LEAVE, GRIEVE

WAR...PLAN

GRAND...SCAM
STRIFE...KNIFE
BLED...RED
YOU'RE...DEAD
KIDS...SAD
NO...DAD
WIFE...GRIEVE
CAN'T...BELIEVE
HUSBAND...HERO
PROSPECTS...ZERO
FUTURE...BLACK
FAITH...ATTACK
HOPE...LEARN
GRIEF...SPURN
COMFORT...YEARN
TO CHRIST....RETURN

ETERNAL PURSUIT

March, 2009

When God designed the heart of man, included in His perfect plan.
A strong attraction, He would leave, she for Adam, he for Eve.
Right up to now, this drive's in play, It's manifesting every day.

This fascinating pirouette, each boy positioning to get,
attention from a lovely rose, he doesn't stand a chance, he knows.
But then one day she throws a glance, he hopes it isn't just by chance.

He chased her while she coyly fled, but let him win…this guy is dead.
For now she leads him by the nose, he follows everywhere she goes.
But gradually, attractions wane…the pirouette begins again.

It's at this juncture, if I may, there's something I would like to say.
This hunger filling young folks hearts, that manifests in fits and
starts,
Is normal, I want you to know, when tied to God's scenario,

God wants to bring some order in, with your permission, let's begin.
Every year God strives to save, each post-pubescent, surging wave.
Apply the brakes, show some restraint, you think you're old
enough?…you aint.

Don't bite that apple, you might find, that half a worm you've left
behind.

Carpenters tell a man that's new, if measured thrice, one cut will do.
A baby always cries, me! me!…But you display maturity?

I know you're charging out the gate, to get that girl, you cannot wait.
But wait a sec, hold on, slow down…wise up, stop acting like a
clown,
Take time to give God time to move, some day an Eve, God will
approve.

So, let's go on with God again, but this time, sing a new refrain.
When God supplies, your perfect Eve, a measure of restraint
achieve.
Let your deportment show respect, while God's instruction,
recollect.

This help-meet, God supplied for life, not to co-habit…for your
wife.
God's given you this precious flower, a choicest bloom, from
heaven's bower.
Entrusted to your tender care, God's blest His children, everywhere.

Just take the time to get to know, her heart's desires, go with the
flow.
You've time to lay foundations well…world without end, the
scriptures tell.
Those well laid plans, good fruit will yield, so settle down, don't
play the field.

WHERE DOES ALL MAN'S WISDOM GO

March, 2009

As the years pile up, my hard-drive inside,
is recording the stuff of life.
For eighty some years, eyes and ears opened wide,
channelled all of life's pleasures and strife.

And now that I've come to the winter of life,
inner peace keeps me joyful each day.
After fifty four years with my lovely wife,
I fly solo since she went away.

But that's not a complaint, she's in heaven now,
we'll be back together one day.
Now I do the cleaning, and cook my own chow,
with some help from a lady I pay.

My white hair is now looking like snow on the roof,
but it's not time to let winter in.
It's now harvest time, and this poetry's proof,
who cares if that snow's getting thin.

I want to keep growing and learning in life,
let surprise and amazement flow.
Why I might even reconcile husband and wife,
who knows where this wisdom might go.

This wonderful station in life's really great,
at my age, there's no need to impress.
Everyone's very kind…understands if I'm late,
And quite helpful if I'm in a mess.

But when a man dies, then all he has learned,
just disappears into thin air,
Could the wisdom contained in his puny brain,
be deposited here somewhere.

Perhaps some wisdom, I can leave when I go,
in the poetry I have amassed.
But a techie's back-up of my inner hard-drive,
Would really give folks quite a blast.

Ecc 12:6 Remember him—before the silver cord is severed, or the golden bowl is broken; before the pitcher is shattered at the spring, or the *wheel* broken at the well,
Ecc 12:7 and the dust returns to the ground it came from, and the spirit returns to God who gave it.

THE WHEEL OF LIFE

July, 2008

The wheel of life moves, at an even pace, one full turn's three score and ten.
If we think of the wheel as 360 degrees, at #1 we appear, but by then,

Mom and Dad move nearer the bottom, say, one hundred and seventy five,
Full of health and strength, and the joy of life, happy to be alive.

But the wheel's inexorably turning, one tiny degree at a time.
As the children grow, the parents will know, past 180, they're starting to climb.

Now, somewhere along this rotation, God is waiting to welcome them in,
To His kingdom and life everlasting, eternal joy they can win.

Then in life, the Lord can anoint them, to save everyone in their
clan.
No one else is positioned to do this, nearly as well as they can.

Then, by God's Grace, they'll take their place, in the phalanx of
Christians strong.
Moving up the degrees, as the Lord they please, teaching family
right from wrong.

As the wheel of life creeps slowly on, we're now past two eighty
four.
Lift a box from it's place, try to run a race, those muscles get really
sore.

But each stage of life, has it's own reward, reflecting how God has
blessed.
Our quiver of arrows, give back to their Moms, so that we're not
overly stressed.

The degrees have arrived at three sixty, the place God said is the
end.
But add ten years plus, if we just stay strong, that's a bonus from
God, my friend.

Now the pointer's ceased from climbing, starts again down the other
side.
We're not nearly the man that we used to be, but we're still the same
inside.

As we look back at life, I must thank my wife, but the glory belongs
to God.
Whatever we did, wherever we went, we were blessed wherever we
trod.

Now, the wheel of life's, turned back to the place, where a baby I
was called.
And some parallels now with the babies I see…like, my head is also
bald.

Mom's are always looking for teeth to appear, while I'd like to see
the same.
The kids need frequent diaper change, I too visit, again and again.

Have you noticed, the babies are always asleep, I too have trouble,
awake to keep.
Whenever they're hungry they want to cry, I know how they feel,
'cause so do I.

But I am, my dear, very happy here, no desire for an earlier age,
With my load of years, and concealing my fears, maybe they'll think
I'm a sage,

I do nothing to discourage the notion, just keep quiet, and stifle my
pride, If I'm careful, then no one will ever know, that it's only me
inside,

When we get to the age where we're 80 plus, pray for help to fulfill
each day,
And don't stake a claim, on each ache and pain, or else they won't
go away,

Look around for a way to help other folk, something you're able to
do,
Something you've never tried before, something completely new,

You'll find that it adds some excitement, a reason to get out of bed,
'Till your wheel of life moves it's last degree, then, surprise…you
wake up dead.

VALENTINE'S POEM

When God created little girls,
He filled them with His Love.

Then stayed with them, through trials and hurts,
watching from above.

Each one...a lovely gift from God,
given unto men.

If these treasures men would only love,
and gently nurture...then,

Men would reap a constant harvest,
of gentle loving care.

A woman's heart is made to love,
...spread blessing everywhere.

May these flowers give you pleasure,
though they'll only last awhile.

A little gift to warm your heart,
just to help you smile.

HAPPY VALENTINE DAY

REAL MEN

June, 2008

What is a Real Man anyway, what is it that makes him unique
As I mentally ruminated I thought, It's the gift of public speak
But then I thought that this can't be, Hitler had that in spades
He was possessed and ordered by Satan…his every act degrades

It must be something else, I thought, maybe having lots of gold
But to give some away would lift him up…lift Jesus up, we're told
Since this goes against God's teaching, then some other attribute
I had to scratch my cranium now, since it's not having, lots of loot

Hey, now I know what the secret is, It's having fancy clothes
But no, that's admiring the outer man, wrong again, I suppose
But a new suit makes him feel real good, with matching tie and shoes
Motivated by desire to flaunt his attire…pride causes him to lose

Ah, now I know the secret, it's attending Church each week
To make the Pastor happy, when he sees him in his seat
'Cause that's the place he always sits, newcomers best beware
That's his place fully paid for, they can find another chair

I've got it now, it's really how, he makes his body fit
He works hard at his exercise, a strong body must be it
He can exercise his body, but must not neglect his soul
To exercise his spirit, with Gods Word, will make him whole

Now, all's okay that went before, God doesn't frown on fun
That's obeying the word that Jesus gave, "Occupy till I come"
The problem's not in life's routine, God tells us that's our part
The problem's in our motives, that's why God looks at our heart

So now I know what a Real Man is, the secret's finally out
My eyes were blind, I couldn't see, they surround me all about
They're really average Christians, with gifts from God who knows
With Christ inside, as they go through life, God's Holy Spirit flows

ROTTEN KIDS, OLD FOGIES

October, 2008

When I look at these kids, their insensitive ways,
They don't seem to care, disrespecting our days.
What in the world's going on in their heads,
If their not raising hell…they're all day in their beds.

When these kids look at us, all they see is distrust,
They think we resent them, would like to pre-empt them.
And maybe we would, 'cause they don't seem to care,
With their sloppy attire, and their strange coloured hair.

But my old creaky heart, smiles inside at the sight,
Of their careless good health and their physical might.
Their skin is so smooth, and their movements so lithe,
Maybe one day those girls could be somebody's wife.

Oh Lord, what's this gulf separating us all,
They're so physically agile, while I'm apt to fall.
Their hearts are so restless, they're searching for what,
While my heart is content, with the truth that I've got.

Is the gift of salvation, in the Bible so clear,
Not enough to content them, and keep them from fear.
The truth is no secret, they've heard it before,
So what's goading them on, like they're looking for war.

In Luke 1:17, John the Baptist was told,
Turn the hearts of the fathers to the children of old.
And turn disobedience to the wisdom of the just,
To prepare for the Lord, he was told that he must.

Lord, please do this to-day, please bring into the fold,
All the restless youth…from out in the cold.
Lord, anoint in our mouths, those words that give life,
Bring those wonderful kids into blessing, from strife.

And help us Oh Lord, their faults to see past,
See their hearts that are starving, for Love that will last.
Forgive me, Oh God, for my critical heart,
Bind us all with Your Love, so we're never apart.

OUR WORLD RENEWED

July, 2008

Today as I sat with my mind disengaged,
And it started to wander, at peace, amazed.
It meandered unbidden down roads of its own,
Roads never traveled…really unknown.

The thoughts that began to take shape in my head,
Opened some issues and led me ahead,
To the place where I wondered, just how would I fare,
When Jesus comes back, will I really be there.,

How will our Lord make such radical change,
In an instant of time, the whole world rearrange.
Then out of my memory, a hint came to light,
I remember He said He would banish the night.

But that still did not settle the issue of man,
Whose heart has been evil since Satan began.
With temptation he schemed and had a good start,
Praise God, Jesus said we would have a new heart.

I now understand just a little bit more, but I'm still in a bind.
It's hard to envision this absolute change, with such a puny mind.
For instance I think of Adam and Eve, did they suffer infirmity?
I know they did not, for when God creates, then perfect they will be.

So then, this question comes to the fore, why are we sickness prone?
Since we're made in the image of God, I ask, why do we suffer
alone?
But then I remember Deut. 28, if Gods laws we disobeyed,
To Gods commandments we will not hark, so consequences
degrade.

That problem's cleared up, so let's get back,
To our future on God's new earth.
Let's try to imagine hearts once so black,
Doing good for all they are worth.

For instance I'm thinking of dollar and cent,
Our medium now of exchange.
In Gods changed world, we won't need it for rent,
All's given away…how strange.

So, I'll go to the butchers to get a chop,
Oops, not anymore, they closed the shop.
There's no meat 'cause nothing on earth can die,
So for dinner we'll feast on apple pie.

Our appetites will undoubtedly change,
Food grown from the ground, God will arrange.
Just like He stated in Genesis one,
We'll grow all our food…won't that be fun.

Everyone is engaged in creative work,
Everyone busy…nobody shirk.
Everything we create we will freely give,
To everyone else, to help them live.

Now everyone's doing the same thing too,
So there's plenty for everyone, not just a few.
Why would there be greed, when all freely take,
From everyone else, the things they make.

Boy, it's hard to imagine, but I'll really try,
Will I live forever, and never die.
Will my heart be filled with Gods great Love,
ill I see Him right here, no longer above.

And the sun and the moon are no longer required,
But what will I do, when I'm really tired?
When I want to sleep, but can't turn off the light,
I know all will be well, God will be my delight.

Then, maybe one day I'll visit the Zoo,
No I won't, 'cause they're no longer there.
Animals are now free to visit you,
They won't hurt us, they really care.

And why would we have to have jails anymore,
When no one does anything bad.
No policemen or judges or armies or war,
And no reason to ever get mad.

As I'm daydreaming still in my little chair,
Consciousness starts to creep in.
My mind returns from that world somewhere,
Back to work I had better begin.

T.V. PRODUCERS GOTTA PRODUCE!

March, 2009

Old and creaky Billy boy, has got to go to bed,
After such a busy day, he's got to rest his head.

Then after he is sound asleep, in comes the little wife,
She's all wired up and falls asleep, subconsciously she's rife,

For subliminal activity…it's crazy night-mare time,
that bedroom get's quite busy, to wake Billy'd be a crime.

Billy really can't join in with her, he doesn't have a script,
Can't co-ordinate his two left feet, when sleeping, getting tripped.

Wakes up tired at five o'clock, has no get-up-and-go,
On hands and knees, crawls to the car, he must produce the show.

His job gets quite intensive, as he labours long and hard,
He's just like a stand up comic, they all say he's quite a card.

He said he's tired and flustered, he's just got to get a grip,
Now he didn't mean it that way so, don't give him any lip.

He's so busy with his little knobs, and switches everywhere,
He's barking orders left and right…in everybody's hair.

Will someone try to hit the lights, you know that's not his job,
Oh lookey here, it might be him…he found another knob.

He's out on the perimeter, and flying all around,
Camera persons keep an eye on him…his feet don't touch the
ground.

He must hold the show together, or from George he'd get what-for,
If he doesn't keep on juggling…he might be out the door.

He's first one in, and last one out, but he heads for home at last,
Hunched o'er the wheel, with bleary eyes, afraid to drive too fast.

But now he's home, crawls up the stairs, they all sit down to eat,
He can't wait to get into his bed, poor Billy's really beat.

So, here we go, they're all tucked in, once more they'll have a ball,
Having fun in Donna's night-mares, maybe…climbing up the wall.

LIFE'S PURPOSE

Bob McCluskey...June, 2008

Do you ever wonder why in life,
we struggle...seem to suffer
We sleep-walk through each boring day...
seek pleasure, pain to buffer
Do you think we might be missing the point,
just manifesting greed
If we'd only look with Jesus eyes,
we'd see others in greater need

Stephen, God's sweet Servant,
brought them all, under conviction
Their response was not repentance,
but a hate inspired affliction
For they dragged him from the city,
shed his blood and brake his bones
They were expert in this practice,
when they stoned you, you stayed stoned

Except when God has other plans,
and Paul's a case in point
When he and his friends in Iconium,
worked wonders in that joint
The Iconiumites sought to worship Paul,
but it quickly turned to ire

They stoned him at the edge of town…
made sure he did expire

Or so they thought, but it came to nought,
their hatred manifested
Even all his friends who gathered round,
to his demise attested
When he started to stir, and got to his feet,
did he say, "now, what was I doing?"
As they wept with relief, I can hear Paul say,
"Lets go, quit that boo-hoo-ing!"

I hear that they tried, to boil John in oil,
It was probably oil from, the olive
Of which they had an abundant supply,
the trees grew right where they all live
The oil would not boil, though they piled on wood,
impatiently trying to hurry him
But God's purpose said no, you'll all have to go,
it's not yet My time to bury him

So they all went away and left John where he lay,
all covered in slippery oil
Did his oily friends flip, did he slip from their grip,
as they squishily recoil
I'm sure rags they'd bring, for the oil that did cling,
which was not of John's creation

At his age he'd be tired, yet his writing's inspired,
in that Bible Book, Revelation

Now, I often wonder…my friend, do you,
why Stephen must die…Saul approved too
When Paul was stoned, a different opinion,
certain to die, but then God had Dominion
John was to boil, God did not acquiesce.
He was chosen to live. Why, can you guess?
Or why did our Lord have to go to the cross,
it seems at first glance, we all suffered loss

But it is not so, His Blood had to be shed,
to purchase Salvation, that's why Jesus Bled
Sacrifice was required, that is the clue,
those going before laid the groundwork for you
It's God who wields power, over life, over death,
He will till all men take their last breath
We must keep on striving, serving our Lord.
Just take that first step, come on, get aboard

THOUGHTS ON WAR

January, 2009

In countless countries…days of yore,
young men were sacrificed to war.
Each generation breeds, it seems,
their evil men with worldly dreams.

Craving power…be like Gods,
wield power until…exposed as frauds.
Their glory flees…they lose their head,
but in their wake…leave countless dead.

Great evil drives the God of War,
The carnage builds…the cannons roar.
God's heart revealed, in Flanders Field,
for peace, when all the church bells pealed.

Then World War Two…fight to survive,
whole cities…'cinerate alive.
Women…children…old and young,
on war's cruel gallows…all were hung.

And now, to bring us up to date,
we face a foe consumed by hate.
Religious hatred fills their heart,
compelled to blow themselves apart.

For now we fight a different foe,
by day, to work their fields they go.
By night, they plant their roadside bombs,
then blend back into faceless throngs.

Yes, this is now a different war,
far different from the ones before.
Our modern spears are well designed,
no living thing, they leave behind.

Anti-tank shell enters here,
blasts through the tank and out the rear.
Killing all, as it goes through,
no living left among the crew.

But tanks they do not have…at hand,
their bombs contrived from contraband.

Our soldiers fly to places far,
to stain the sands of Kandahar.
Arriving there in vibrant bloom,
for mindless bullets to consume.

Or blinding…blasting…bursting bomb,
a flash of truth…then life is gone.
Young man so vital…full of life,
while back at home…a grieving wife.

Or mother, sister, sweetheart dear,
she can't be with him, over hear.
An Honour Guard attends the plane,
until at last, he's home again.

Highway of Heroes…His last Mile,
on bridges overhead, meanwhile.
The people stand with faces grim,
salute, and wave "Adieu" to him.

God's likeness laid beneath the sod,
David said…"dead can't praise God".
Winged angels hover overhead,
to succour them, the righteous dead.

Then souls of men, escorted by,
God's angels, up to God on high.
Where pain and tears are finally past,
Eternity with God…at last.

We judge our leaders…think we know,
the truth…from information flow.
But information's oft untrue,
deception flows…to me and you.

Back home, they demonstrate for peace,
and shout, "this killing has to cease".
A perfect world would cede their will,
then men would never, others kill.

Imperfect though, this world will stay,
till Jesus comes, to have His way.
While Satan's evil plagues our life,
embroiling us in endless strife.

If all men now, were filled with Love,
from God in heaven, up above.
Then all the world, in Jesus name,
would love each other…all the same.

Men killing men, could never be,
no fear or hate, by God's decree.
The answer then, seems very clear,
men must seek Jesus, far and near.

To bring His Peace then, we must pray,
God, change men's hearts, no other way.
Lord, with Your Spirit, fill all men,
then Peace will fill Your world…again.

EVEN SO, COME LORD JESUS.

QUESTIONS, QUESTIONS, QUESTIONS

November, 2008

Sometimes when my mind ventures out on its own,
My fuzzy thoughts, become questions full blown.
The seeds of confusion begin to be' sown.
Can these questions be answered, I ask with a groan.

Why am I thinking these questions so deep,
Causing head to ache and keep me from sleep.
Is there really a God who will cause me to reap,
From my actions, a harvest…a destiny keep.

Is there really a heaven, and really a hell?
Was there really a Satan, from heaven fell?
Can he keep me from God, and under his spell?
Can he ruin my life…is that sulphur I smell?

But am I not the one, my own choices to make?
Do I not decide, which direction life takes?
It's all about me…I'm the one with the stake.
Oh, why did I start this…it keeps me awake.

I'm a pretty good guy, I don't do nothin' wrong.
Maybe have a few drinks, or sing a few songs.
So surely not hell…heaven's where I belong.
Wouldn't I be at home, midst the heavenly throng?

What's that you say, that I don't qualify.
You're not telling me true, I think it's a lie.
Why can't I come in, please explain to me why?
My good deeds outweigh bad, I'm a pretty good guy.

I believe there's a God, who's running the show,
Watching me from above, so look out below.
What you say makes me nervous, fear starts to grow.
I feel very exposed…the sweat starts to flow.

Please help me; I need you to show me the way.
The way is a person?…is that what you say?
The person is Jesus?…to Him I must pray?
Are you sure that He'll hear me…will He let me stay?

Ok, now I'm ready…please show me the way,
Ok Jesus, it's me, I'm not sure what to say.
Yes! I'm a sinner, and I'm sorry today.
Come in Jesus, and save me…is that how to pray?

Oh wow! I feel different, so happy and clean.
I now feel so forgiven…now I know what you mean.
Works won't get me to heaven…Christ has to redeem.
I must tell all my friends…that it isn't a dream.

THE MATING GAME

March, 2009

Boy...Age, 18.
Words falter, fail, expression lack,
Her sweetness to extol.
If e'er such loveliness looks back,
How will I keep control.

I'm sure she'd never feign to see,
Or even deign to know.
One lacking charm and wit, like me.
So little promise, show.

I must be mad, to even think,
That I could stand a chance,
Miss loveliness in white and pink,
Must look on me askance.

Miss Loveliness...Age, 17.
Why does he look at me like that,
He's just a geeky kid.
Why does he wear that funny hat,
I'm glad I ran and hid.

7 years later, they meet...Boy, single...now Vice-President
Why, Hello! You look quite familiar,
Didn't I know you in school?
To himself...(she's even lovelier),
(I was such a fool).

Girl, single...now President
Why yes, I do remember now,
Weren't you a year ahead?
To herself...(he's really different...wow),
(I think his name was Fred).

Boy...hungrily
I'm off to lunch...you too...that's great,
Why not have lunch with me.
We'll eat right here, won't keep you late,
See where it leads...agree?

This story long, we'll just keep brief,
The wedding bells were chimed.
Now President, he's been made Chief,
Miss Loveliness...resigned.

ANGELS

March 2008

How exciting to know, that our Lord loves us so,
while all-knowing, right from the beginning.
He made this provision to soften the blow
of Satan, to keep him from winning.

God gave to each one,
born under His Son
an impressive Angelic being.
Though we're unaware, he's always there,
With the Holy Spirit agreeing.

He'll be my defense, he'll direct my ways.
He's always involved in giving God praise.
And he'll never leave me all of my days.
I can almost see him grinning.

Now I know that myriads of Angels exist.
Everywhere, on eternities maps.
But I'd sure like to know where the Angels go
when there's nothing to do
for a decade or two
Does eternity cancel times gaps?

And I know from God's Word that Angels can fight
Michael helped as they battled twenty one days
'gainst an angel of darkness, these Angels of Light
Fought the Prince of Persia who caused them delays.
God's Angels respond as Daniel prays
and battle with all their might.

So I asked myself, myself, said I,
as my mind sees Angels at war in the sky,
and this question entered my feeble mind,
what weapons are used, the explosive kind?
Or mounted on horses they charge to the fray,
wielding great swords, each other to flay?
Or hand to hand combat, to grapple and grip,
with enormous strength each other to flip?

I think that's as far as this silliness goes.
They're spirit, not flesh and blood.
God's Angels use light to defeat their foes.
Not Darth Vader's lightsword, as everyone knows.
But the presence of God, as His Righteousness flows,
And they're swept away, like a flood.

Although we're aware, God's Angels are strong,
that their might over ours is much greater.
But in God's word we're told
that to worship is wrong,
the creation, instead of Creator.

Angels can never, all powerful be,
or always, everything know.
They cannot at the same time,
everything see.
In a moment of time, everywhere be.
Simultaneously everywhere go.
Only God can.

By the power of God, they're allowed to appear
for a task they're ordained to perform.
For men, when they've entertained strangers, it's clear,
have entertained Angels unawares.
Sacrificially helping another man's cares,
they've helped Angels in human form.

Now once again in my feeble mind
my imagination's running wild.
What in the world do the Angels eat,
dare I ask like a little child?
Does they're Manna bland
need a helping hand,
Maybe spices to give it some heat.
'Cause nothing in Heaven can ever die,
for sure, there won't be any meat.

Do they ever gather at each others house
for a social evening together

To listen to music, enjoy some Strauss,
Or gather in groups, though never to grouse.
To maybe discuss the weather.

Are they able to dance when a waltz is played?
Do the carpets and furniture ever get frayed?
And where in the world does that stuff get made?
Are their comforters stuffed with feathers?

When they travel from heaven to earth, I try,
to imagine their speed, just the blink of an eye.
While a U.F.O., unable to vie,
must stare bug eyed, as Angels flash by.
They'll rush to their fuel tank to see if it's dry.
And then check their engine together.

We are also informed
that in heaven they show,
a great deal of emotion
as soon as they know,
that a sinner is saved
for great joy is displayed.
Dare I ask in what way it's addressed?
Do they jump in the air with athletic flair?
Do they give them a hand?
Do they strike up the band?
Just how's their emotion expressed?

Now I've asked many questions, as everyone knows,
from a natural perspective I fear.
Never got around to talk about clothes.
Never opened the subject of buttons and bows.
Or of absolute zero that's found out in space.
If I go any farther, I may need Grace.
In my heart, a command to stop, I hear.
To conclude this now, has become quite clear.
So it's time to say goodby,

SHALOM

March, 2009

It would really be nice, when I greet my friends,
To wish them completeness of life.
To proclaim the blessings that God intends,
To be free from fear and strife.

Tranquility, and adequate wealth,
for all the rest of their days.
To live their lives in radiant health,
God's blessings in multiple ways.

In return, it would be a wonderful thing,
If their response would also be.
To wish all of these blessings that God can bring,
On the head of little old me.

Now, the Hebrew people, wherever they are,
Seem always to land on their feet.
They prosper despite being scattered far,
Through whatever distress they meet.

Death and life are in, the power of the tongue,
Do you think this could be a clue?
These blessings they wish on old and young,
If we could only be that way too.

This variety of blessings, each time we meet,
Would take an impossible time.
We'd be standing and blessing with aching feet,
Isn't loitering a classified crime?

But the light just went on…I know how it's done.
It's so simple, it's really absurd.
When they speak SHALOM on everyone,
All that blessing's in one little word.

Whether coming or going, they're Shalom-ing away,
And those blessings from God they believe.
So now we can SHALOM each other all day,
Then those blessings we too will receive.

SHALOM!

FREE WILL

November, 2002

How awesome to know, that each of our lives,
as we live them, are moving along,

a path we believe to be chosen by us,
could it be that we're terribly wrong.

Is the way that we go, the unknowing result,
of a plan that was made long ago,

by our wonderful God, who with infinite love,
the beginning and end, would know.

As we move through life, and our influence falls,
on others who cross our path,

do we leave with them, do they leave with us,
a reason to cry or to laugh,

as an intricate part of His unknown plan,
of Gods destiny, we must keep,

unknowingly moving from soul to soul,
of the harvest that God will reap.

But of course we know, there is more than this,
for God granted us free will.

It's impossible yet to understand,
how our choices add grist to Gods mill.

But this we know, of this we are sure,
if Christ is alive in our heart,

We're assured of eternity worshiping God.
From His Kingdom, we'll never depart.

HEROES

May, 2008

What claim to fame, could somebody make
What accomplishment able, the world to shake
That would register high, in the minds of men
At the top on a scale of, say, 1 to 10

Would you think of the one who invented the wheel
As a worthy candidate…how would you feel
Or maybe the man who created fire
Do you think he could possibly rate much higher

Or what of the man who invented the clock
Whose mind was inspired, as he went for a walk
As he thought of dividing up daylight and dark
To hours, minutes and seconds, just for a lark

And then, bringing our focus more up to date
To a modern researcher you might relate
The inventor of electrical power could be one
If you touch those two wires, it won't be fun

What else can we think of, computers perhaps
For their speed in computing, our minds can't match
Each year they go faster, they make quite a splash
Each new one's much better, but then it goes "crash"

There are other mind bending, earth shaking things
Like the man who successfully gave us wings
And we fly through the air, many miles in a flash
But just like computers, they too can crash

Now, I know that this subject can have no end
So I'll get to the point, while you're still my friend
I'm about to reveal who's accomplished the highest
And I won't hide the truth, 'cause I'm really quite biased.

In Mark 8:36 Jesus makes it quite clear
By this statement, He banished all heroes, held dear
Every hero we think of, must come to a stop
Though he struggle and strive, he can't get to the top

But there are many heroes, not only just one
Who have faltered not, in the race that they run
Who quietly labour, to obey God's command
They bring men to Salvation, in every land

So, because Jesus said, that one soul's beyond price
And will live forever, have Eternal Life
Since one soul's worth more than the whole world, then
All these heroes of God, rate much more than a 10

This all puts the lie, to so much we hold dear
Where truth really lies, has become very clear
So Lord, help us to value, the things you reveal
To do what you command us, not just what we feel

VALENTINE FOR JESUS

February, 2009

We love you, dear Jesus, our Saviour, our Lord,
Your love's ever selfless, our love seeks reward.

A Valentine wish, from our hearts, incomplete,
From hearts that are hungered, from passion so weak.

Our hearts wistful for heaven, way up where You are,
Though You also abide in our hearts…You're not far.

We've assurance dear Lord, You do hear our hearts speak,
Does our yearning reach heaven, though our cries are so weak?

How exciting to know, that one day we will be,
Up in heaven…that day our Lord Jesus, we'll see.

Only then we will know, even as we are known,
Our perception complete, when in heaven, we're home.

Lord, our Valentine hearts, are the ones You exchanged,
For our stony hearts when, our life You rearranged.

With a love so forgiving, You cleansed all our sin,
Now our cup is so full, it flows over the brim.

Sp Lord, from our hearts, here's a Valentine wish,
Please make us the channels, You use to furnish,

The rewards Luke six tells us, that You'll have men pour,
Into bosoms of those, who showed bounty before.

PROMISED CHANGE

January 2009

U.S. President's election, we saw Barak Obama win.
The masses seemed to fall in love, with his charismatic grin.
I know that he has been declared, a Christian all his life.
Michelle I'm sure would claim the same, to be his Christian wife.

I really can't imagine, why he'd want that Cat-Bird seat,
All the current major problems, 'gonna knock you off your feet.
If not dealing with the terrorists, or propping up the banks,
It's restarting the economy, and he won't get any thanks.

Will he legislate a new beginning, in the automotive plants,
To get the nation off of oil, by increasing all the grants.
To motivate research designed to change to hydrogen,
This whole new source of power, would employ so many men.

Just go on a wartime footing, jump right in with all we've got,
why even in a year or two, it could really change a lot.
Our dependence on that liquid gold, from the middle east,
would slow down to a trickle, break that yoke to say the least.

Now, we'll always have a need for oil…in plastics, just for one,
but we have enough at home for that, we've really just begun.
This would staunch the major flow of wealth, out to foreign lands,
If these trillions stayed at home…we'd hold our future in our hands.

With a hydrogen economy, air pollution would improve,
if we're causing global warming, then there's not much time to lose.
We know that hydrogen is plentiful, but a problem to extract,
but we've found a non polluting way, to get it…that's a fact.

A new, small, Pebble Bed Reactor, high temperature, gas cooled,
factory produced, shipped anywhere, technicians can be schooled.
It can never have a meltdown…there's no water to corrode,
specks of uranium in graphite balls…there's nothing to explode.

The enormous cost of a reactor, is reduced dramatically,
for electricity and hydrogen, and it's all pollution free.
The lifetime of expended fuel's a fraction of the years,
that current nuclear waste requires, this cancels lots of fears.

So it seems that all the factors, are now sitting there in place,
the only thing that's now required, is the will to start the race.
If Obama can defeat, the vested interests that oppose,
he'll be everybody's hero…bring oil's era to a close.

PROSPER! NOT JUST SURVIVE!

March, 2009

The strongest, richest nation that all history did record,
lives a few miles to our south…the U.S.A.
In history it is written, they were founded in the Lord,
and the Lord has blessed them…right up to today.

The founders of our nation, very godly men as well,
recorded God's dominion…set in stone.
Together, both our nations have been ringing freedoms bell,
as we've staunchly stood together…not alone.

We've fought in wars together, grew in peacetime fellowship,
and come down the years together as great friends.
It would be quite true to tell you, we're connected at the hip,
we're rock solid, and we trust it never ends.

As Christians, we are quite aware, that Christ will come again,
Just before He comes, events will be severe.
Our economies' are shaking, causing great financial pain,
And this circumstance elicits massive fear.

But again, because we're Christians, we well know in whom we trust,
Where our treasure is, that's where our heart will be.
Our faith must be rock steady, in a boom, or in a bust.
What we do with our resources…that's the key.

If we focus on financial needs, we'll never have enough,
And we scramble, so our little ships won't sink.
If God feeds the little sparrows, get our focus off of stuff,
he'll be sure to feed us also…don't you think.

The Israelites in Egypt, stayed apart in Goshen land,
from the plagues that came, God's mercy kept them free.
Just like us, they were God's people, covered by His Hand,
and He'll do the same for us…for you and me.

So our very best insurance, if it's coming from our heart,
Is, increase our giving, show in God we trust.
God loves a cheerful giver, when our finances depart,
Know that God's Word will not fail us…that's a must.

God said He'd build His Church, and He lets us help Him too,
'cause He wants us to be with Him, that's His will.
That's how we lay our treasure up in heaven, me and you,
And even when we fail, He loves us still.

LOVE DIVINE

March, 2009

Ah, sweetest love, to young hearts brings,
pure thoughts of flowers…of lovely things.
What grander force, to conquer thee,
than loves long suff'ring ecstasy.

Give lover's hearts…sweet fragile flowers,
dominion o'er all mankind's hours.
Then man fulfill his days with love,
in tribute to our Lord above.

Life giving Son, with love so warm,
embracing roses, bloom and thorn.
Their copious bounty, lovely hue,
Sweet perfume, to once more renew.

Impatient roses…unfulfilled,
with hungry love, their weeping stilled.
Embrace Son's warmth, with petals spread,
Loves fragrance fill…His garden bed.

For every rose, with fragrance rife,
rejoicing in eternal life.
Will blossom in God's garden, planned,
sweetly perfume, His promised land.

Remember, God one day revealed,
that God is Love, His Word unsealed.
His greatest love, interred in earth's,
cold darkened womb…sweet roses birth.

How lovely when God's Love o'rpowers,
life's darkness, loosing virtue's flowers.
For God does e'er bestow on man,
forgiving love…fulfilling plan.

LIFE-DEATH CYCLE

April, 2009

How can we ever, even try,
when full of life, with death to vie.
When life is pulsing through each vein,
our hearts, from thoughts of death, abstain.

Death so abhorrent, death so vile,
no more to love, no more to smile.
But death will win, soon, now or then,
no one can prophesy just when.

Young bodies, lovely, made to flaunt,
so full of life, so full of want.
Young flesh so firm, contained within,
such healthy, glowing, flawless skin.

And then one day, we don't know why,
when life departs, those bodies die.
How can such beauty, so degrade,
the head reducing to the blade.

The blade reducing to the stem,
the stems vague memory of when,
from earth it came, small seed implant.
Remember life before…it can't.

And so, life's reel, so soon rewound,
sweet life, replanted in the ground.
But lifeless now, can't reproduce,
new life again, no living juice.

And then that lover, death embraced,
we almost seem afraid to face.
Such degradation, we must flee,
for one day soon, 'twill beckon me.

HEBREWS, CHAPTER ONE

March, 2009

Our Father God, in centuries past, spoke through the prophets old,
God's mysteries were not revealed to people then, we're told.
But wonder of all wonders, God to-day has sent His Son,
and now the Bible clearly tells, all truth, to everyone.

What a startling testimony to creation of the worlds,
in Hebrews chapter one, the Lordship of God's Son unfurls.
In verse two, these last days God, has spoken clearly by His Son.
In verse nine, with oil of gladness, He's made Lord of everyone.

In verse ten, the earths foundations, laid by Jesus Christ's commands,
and creation of the heavens, wondrous works by Jesus hands.
In verse eleven, all creation, as a vesture, will wax old,
but the years of Jesus Christ, our Lord, will never fail, we're told.

In verse three, our Father God revealed, in revelation sure,
Christ, the brightness of His glory, and image of His person, pure.
When seeing Christ in Scripture…Heavenly Father is revealed.
By embracing Christ with hearts of truth, our sin is now repealed.

In verse eight, addressing Christ the Son, Thy throne will ever last,
Thy sceptre is of righteousness, now, future and times past.
God never said to angels, come, and at My right hand sit,
only to His righteous Son, this throne He would commit.

That's not to discount angels, wondrous creatures God has made,
in verse fourteen, ministering spirits who, of nothing are afraid.
God has sent them forth to minister to, salvation's heirs, we're told,
so, with ministering angels all around, how can I not be bold.

Now, won't you please allow me, since I'm trying to be bold,
to adjure you…turn to Hebrew's one, if your heart is feeling cold.
With open book, revealing look, back to when time began,
when Father, Son and Holy Spirit, first created man.

HEAVEN'S NURSERY

Bob McCluskey...March, 2009

Have you ever conjectured, on all of the lives,
that are taken away by abortion,
Multitudes of sweet babies, who never saw life,
whatever now is their portion.

Or the hearts of the ill-advised mothers to be,
how later in life, they've all fared,
Many were really just children themselves,
reacting from feeling so scared.

Hungry for love, they'd only get...
moments of passion...lifetime of regret,
After abortion, to weep in the night,
and wonder about their babies plight.

Has our Lord made provision in heaven above,
somewhere for those babies to go,
Also, all of the families killed in war,
multitudes He would know.

There's no place in this poem, for me to relate,
the horrors of man's genocide,
It's all too heartless to even think,
that's for God, not me, to decide.

Father, Christ cried, as He hung on the Cross,
forgive, they know not what they do,
Thinking not of Himself, but the far road ahead…
forgiveness for me and for you.

Now, the story that I'm describing here…
imagination on my part,
Not much is based on the Word of God,
it's mostly out of my heart.

I like to think, in these mothers hearts,
that repentance has ever flown,
Mom will go to heaven, then God will match,
each child to the Mom of it's own.

And now in this nursery in heaven,
they'll enjoy their mothers breast,
To drink the sweetest mother's milk,
in mother's arms find rest.

I like to think that this is something,
our loving Lord might do,
To heal these precious mother's hearts…
I know I would, would you?

Why their might even be a sand box,
where dirt's allowed to stay,

Where little kids have lots of fun…
while in the dirt they play.

And then at night, a mother's wish,
will swish them nice and clean,
Their mother's love will tuck them in,
to have a Jesus dream.

And won't it be just wonderful,
when those frightened little girls,
Who had their child aborted,
can admire their children's curls.

They can now fulfill their mother heart,
pour out their mother love,
On their precious little baby…
in God's nursery up above.

GOD'S JUDGMENT SEAT

December, 2008

There are many today, who on earth walk away,

From God's Word when they hear it expounded.

But not you, and not me, surely that could not be,

When God's death knell for sin has resounded.

Many men, down the road, when they leave their abode,

The last time…their last journey on earth;

Will no longer rejoice, with their beverage of choice,

No more alcohol served in a hearse.

There are many today, who with certitude say,

Live it up, we've got no one to thank.

When death comes it's the end, nothing follows, my friend,

There's no God, just eternity blank.

Or if God's real, as you say, He won't turn me away;

If God's Love…it's like cash in the bank.

That last line's really true, God does love me and you,

Longs to see us set free from sin's pale.

For His Love is so deep, gave His Son just to keep,

The whole world from eternal travail.

So God has made a way, please hear what we say,

You'll be saved, death will not be the end.

Receive Jesus today, with the devil don't stay,

Then we'll see you in Heaven, my friend.

Let's go along, with this profligate throng,

beyond eternity's gates.

If we'll trust in God's word, He'll expose the absurd;

At God's judgment, let's see what awaits.

Jesus spoke of a rich man, tormented in hell,

Crying out to Abraham, wanting to tell,

His five brothers, a warning about this place;

If one came from the dead, the truth they'd embrace.

But Abraham said, if God's Word they reject,

Sending Lazarus from heaven, would have no effect.

And God makes every effort to warn us today,

Just believe in His Word, it's the only way.

Getting back to our friends, it's now judgment time,

As they're waiting their turn, in that fearful line.

Then, when their turn comes, and they stand before God,

Angels open God's book, we hear heaven applaud.

They're beginning to read, every shameful account;

The man starts to protest, that's too high an amount.

Lord, when did we see you, hungry and sick,

And not feed you and help you, this must be a trick.

God said, when you gave not, to the least of these,

You were selfish and greedy, you'd watch them freeze.

You said, welfare and food banks will help them along.

You said, I need my money…I can't help this throng.

Then the Judge of all men, as He was about,

To pronounce His judgment…said, cast the man out,

From My presence, to endless fire down beneath.

Led away with great weeping and gnashing of teeth.

There is no escape, God must be obeyed,

All the screams and the heat, make him very afraid.

Too late to repent, no communion here,

Separation from God…indescribable fear.

In this sulfur he's burning, yet never consumed,

Isolated…alone…he's eternally doomed.

But let's back up the tape, to where Heaven awaits,

With a different scenario.

Let's now see him choose Christ, to redeem his life,

Praise God, now to Heaven he'll go.

Oh Lord, we're so thankful, for when we believed,

How heavy our hearts, for so many deceived.

Oh Lord, we rejoice in the Blood and the Cross,

We're your children forever, we'll not suffer loss.

MY LOVELY MARGARET

March 29/2008...8.00pm

I'll always remember Marg's faith at the end,
her sweet spirit as life ebbed away.
Although now I'm alone, still on God I'll depend,
'till at last we're together one day.

I'm certain our love will endure beyond time,
while I serve God on earth till the end.
I can only imagine her wonder sublime,
in the presence of Jesus, her friend.

I treasure the gift of her love in my life,
and for making our marriage secure.
I'll always be grateful to God for my wife,
who was ever so faithful and pure.

The family and friends that Marg's leaving behind,
in this life, have been blessed by her giving.
And I know that remembering, many will find,
much joy to have shared in her living.

So we all are not saying goodbye to my wife,
but simply, "till next time we meet".
We'll carry on here, just living our life,
'till my sweetheart, in heaven, we greet.

Your loving husband
Bob McCluskey

AGAIN, MARGARET MY DARLING

March, 2009

Margaret my darling, can it really be,
a whole year since your smile, I was able to see.
It is true what they say, time is able to heal,
but deep in my heart, your sweet love I still feel.

At times when my thoughts wander back to that day,
to the moment we parted, when you went away,
back up to God, who loaned you to me.
Did angels escort you…just what did you see?

When I think of Elijah, second Kings we are told,
a different departure, for this prophet of old.
A whirlwind took him up, from earth, still alive.
Did God quickly transform him, so he could survive?

Of course all these answers, are hidden from man,
God has not yet revealed, every part of His plan.
But I try to imagine, your wonderment when,
Jesus welcomed you home, back to heaven again.

When I let my mind wander, and think of you there.
I wonder my sweet, if your still aware,
of our life together, or what's happening now.
If there's some way to tell, I sure wish I knew how.

God says He has wiped every tear from your eye,
so I know that you'll not be unhappy, or cry.
You're now able to eat from the Tree of Life,
I'm no longer your husband, and you're not my wife.

And there's not any difference from daylight to night,
that's all part of time, not eternity…right?
God said you now know, even as you are known.
Does this mean you now know what I'm doing at home?

Just in case then, I'd better keep everything neat,
And clean up after cooking, or grinding my wheat.
Cause you know that I use it, for baking my bread,
and I'd better be sure, to each day make my bed.

But one day all this fuss here on earth, I'll escape,
to be up there with you, and have no bed to make.
So look for me Honey, I'll be coming your way,
I'll be looking for you…on arrival one day.

JESUS LOVES ME

March, 2008

Jesus loves me, this I know,
  for the Bible tells me so.
Repentant blasphemer, a fool,
  blind to truth, break every rule.
Yes Jesus loves me, the Bible tells me so
  Self indulgent, greedy glutton,
    expanded belly pops a button.
Closet stuffed with surplus shrouds,
  indifferent to the shivering crowds.
Yes Jesus loves me, the Bible tells me so
  Scratch and scramble every penny,
    all for me, you don't get any.
Why should I give you a loan,
worked hard for mine, go get your own.
Yes Jesus loves me, the Bible tells me so
I've banked enough in this account,
  a new one for the next amount.
I'll soon have more than I can spend,
  enough to see me to the end.
Yes Jesus loves me, the Bible tells me so
That Jesus died for such a one,
who from the truth would always run.
The outer man's all we would see,
  but Jesus saw the heart of me.

Yes Jesus loves me, the Bible tells me so
He reached my heart with touch divine,
to save my soul, and just in time.
Oh God, You snatched me out of hell,
I give you all, take me as well.

Yes, Jesus loves me, yes, Jesus loves me,
Yes, Jesus loves me, the Bible tells me so!

HOME COOKIN'

March, 2009

Now that I'm without me wife, I'm fendin' for me'self,
So what is all the fuss about, because I'm on the shelf.
All of this palaver, 'bout the work that women do,
I can do it standin' on me head, while makin' Irish stew.

I'll just chop me up some carrots, throw a turnip in as well,
Add a little barley to the pot, and give it time to swell.
Some 'tater's and some celery, now, what else does it need,
Wish me wife was here to help me, I'd pick up a little speed.

Now I'll add a pail of water, gotta get it from the well,
Add a little salt and pepper, just how much, I cannot tell.
Well, here we goes, I'll throw some in, and fan it with me hat,
If I'm runnin' into trouble, I can always call on Pat.

It would be nice if Margaret, could return for just a while,
Not to do the cookin' though, just to see her smile.
Oh, I would accept some cookin' tips, if she was of a mind,
Just to make her think she's helpin', find the things I cannot find.

So, a splash of this, a pinch of that, I'm gonna get it right,
If me friend Pat doesn't like it, then there's gonna be a fight.
It's been bubblin and boilin on the stove for quite a while
I knew that I could do it, lovely beef stew, Irish style.

BEEF! am I in trouble, please Lord, I need relief,
I thought I had it perfect, but I left out all the beef.
I've been choppin' all the fire wood, to keep the fire hot,
me legs are sore from standin' all day long, to stir the pot.

Now, this Irish stew tastes awful, hafta give it to the pig,
Good thing I'm not a drinker, or I'd have a little swig.
Here I thought that all Marg's cookin', was like rollin' off a log,
The only good that comes from this...I have a happy hog.

So, it's pork and beans for supper, I can see her smilin' now,
she knows I've learned me lesson, when I bragged that I knew how.
I had better study cookin', this is not a happy life,
If me dinners don't improve...I'm off to court another wife.

WOMAN

February, 2008

In the Genesis of God's, loving Self revelation,
He began to part the curtains on the stage of time.
Progressively revealing all the wonders of creation,
as the setting for the zenith of His Will Divine.

"Let us make man and woman in our image and our likeness"
This crowning achievement's in His Word displayed.
God wanted many children to be just like Jesus,
to place them in dominion over all He'd made.

Now it's easy for my mind to see God's likeness made in man,
but seeing God as woman, has a different complexion.
God's Word proclaims however, that it's central to His plan,
His image is in woman too, you'll pardon the correction.

So man leaves home and mom and dad, and gladly takes a wife,
who's presence brings a joy and peace, that gives him great elation.
A woman's presence in his home, adds pleasure to his life,
then childbirth partners her with God, to join in His creation.

And how could it be otherwise, since God, who loves us all,
created man and then began, from man, to woman make.
In sweetness and in beauty, men's hearts she would enthrall,
And all was well, but then from hell, there came that cursed snake.

But over time God worked in man, his restoration plan,
to bring us through the centuries, with Christ, back to the fold.
And let there no confusion be, it's woman, not just man,
for woman's part is major, in the oldest story told.

In God's design of woman, he was careful to enclose,
that tender loving influence, without which we'd descend,
to selfish brute depravity, as God most surely knows.
Without her, man could not fulfill, God's determined end.

Make no mistake, in women we're exposed to God's sweet Love.
For, all Godly women, who in life we come across,
reflect God's love and purity, it's coming from above.
Their sacrificial love reflecting, Christ upon the cross.

A MUSICAL GOOD MORNING

March, 2009

Somewhere in the world,
at any moment of our day,
the morning sun spreads living light,
to kiss the night away.
Somewhere a gentle morning mist,
is dissipated…when,
soft colours from God's pallet flood,
o'er mount…o'er glade…o'er glen.

And the danger of the night,
from which small creatures have to hide,
recedes back into darkness,
where by day they must abide.
At any given time…somewhere,
sweet little birds awake,
at golden light of morning,
their first musical to make.

By their millions to the sky they launch,
their colours mock the night,
in the full bloom of their beauty,
as we watch them take to flight.
Each graceful singing creature,
like a music note airborne,

each note adding to the symphony,
a string…a lute…a horn.

So exquisitely perfected…
designed to be just right,
to live their programmed destiny,
radiant in the light.
Then as the sun begins to set,
they know they now must hide,
another day's declining,
as they settle down outside.

They find a perch, keep very still,
try not to make a sound,
for through the night, their enemies,
are prowling all around.
But thankfully, birds multiply,
it's wonderful to know,
At dusk, they softly harmonize,
with sunset's golden glow.

GOD'S FINAL VICTORY

Feb. 2008

Pilgrims fleeing religious persecution in England...1620
Forget Europe! Look West! Your vision keep clear! New Jerusalem
see! Give up everything dear!
Hearts full of song! Burning with zeal! To establish God's
Kingdom! Be stronger than steel!
To count everything joy serving God was their lot, as through raging
storms for this New Land they fought!
Through long days and nights, never counting the cost, 'till at last
they landed, praise God, they're not lost.
And then over time as their settlements grew, righteousness was
established in Jerusalem New.
Then the years rolled by and Satan found hearts, where he brought in
sin with his fiery darts.
Now the passage of time brings us up to today, and we're saddened
to see how much sin brings decay.
Many homes are engulfed by the filth on T.V., and in uncounted
households, destruction we see.
When a baby is born full of sweetness and love, and begins a life
journey that's planned from above.
While yet barely a child, Satan launches his plan, and slips in the
temptations before he's a man.
And if raised in the nurture of parents mature, he'll be trained to
resist and to keep his heart pure.
But if parents are lost and don't know the way, their example at

home will allow him to stray.

To consort with men who call evil good, who revel in darkness, not light as they should.

And as sin drags him closer to hell's heartless gate, we must pray he'll awaken before it's too late.

Satan's plan, so cruel for that babe in the womb, so secure and safe, unaware of his doom.

The abortionist's tool, or a chemical vile, invades his safe haven, injecting foul bile.

Try to think of the horror, millions each year, doomed in the womb, where their trust is so dear.

As our Lord hears their screams, as He weeps for these lost, Heartbrokenly counting the terrible cost.

For these gifts that He's giv'n from heaven above, are rejected, without any sense of His Love.

To be tossed in the fire and rendered to ash, or thrown on the garbage, or parts sold for cash.

Now consider again, and consider we must, that same child attacked by a spirit of lust.

As a man who's consumed by a hunger for flesh, seduces this innocent child at his rest.

So as men seduce men, hearts burning with lust, their minds become reprobate, sinning they must.And God, the designer of conjugal love, is mocked by this ravening seen from above.

While government heads are so slow to make laws, that will end this charade, that have teeth in their jaws.

Don't they know that when Israel went far astray, God's chastening came, as for sin they must pay.

And since out of Love, God with Israel dealt, in our dear Lord for us, could less Love be felt?

So look to the East!!! Is that thunder we hear! Or dust from the masses approaching we fear!

Sound the alarm!!! See that numberless score! They're beginning to stir! Are they marshaled for war!

They serve a strange God who commands them to kill, everyone who refuses to bow to their will.

Every gate to our nations is under attack, while the courage our leaders require, suffers lack,

What machines for destruction and black hearted moles, have already entered to hide in their holes?

Awaiting the signal they know is to come, to then unleash destruction on everyone.

To obey their false god, their own blood blindly spill, we must pray to Lord Jesus, for save us He will.

What now enables, those multitudes poor, who see in our freedom, an opportune lure?

Why, the treasure that's buried deep under their ground, that oil is the glorious wealth they've found.

'Cause our thirst for that oil simply cannot be sated, they're happy to sell it for prices inflated.

The wealth that we've built is now flowing their way, for Satan's deception, they'll use it to pay.

And the temples now seen everywhere in the West, are paid for by oil, at their leader's behest.

As the building continues apace in our lands, not for peace but for conquest, we sit on our hands.

This conspiracy's fruit is apparent world wide, where their critics for fear have to run and to hide.

As hordes of adherents are directed to rampage, murder and mayhem they use to advantage.

As the purpose of God is played out in our land, and as those without God, hold a hopeless hand.

The faithful of God pray with hearts that burn, with fervent belief in our Lord's return.

A great harvest of souls will be reaped at the last, for the time of waiting is almost past.

Men's hearts failing for fear as nature explodes, and self confident godlessness erodes.

Look again to the East!!! We see burning a light, repelling a darkness far deeper than night.

Surrounded by nations that thirst for their blood, God's little Israel held back the flood.

As foretold in the Bible, God answered His call, He replanted His Nation, a beacon to all.

More incredible still, many times without number, attacks rooted in hate, try to catch them in slumber.

But our glorious God moved with might in their midst, with their backs to the wall, He helped them resist.

With God on their side, against impossible odds, hordes attacked with a rallying cry to their gods.

So they raced to the ramparts, their lives on the line, praying to God their response was on time

In the natural, their numbers did not have a chance, as the blood thirsty hordes made a rapid advance.

But they fought in the Spirit, and time after time, inexplicable
victories helped hold the line.

Oh, they did suffer loss, young men's blood had to flow, but God
ordered destruction on many more foe.

As Field Officers faces by God were aglow, they made tactical
moves that helped victory grow.

Victory so complete, that the world intervened, to enforce a false
truce, by their enemies schemed.

Why our Almighty God, who by speaking a word, in an empty and
endless expanse could be heard. Unleashing explosive, cataclysmic
force, designed all creation from secret source.

Why God in the portals of heaven above, also purposed that man
would exist…was it Love?

Why, since knowing all things as only God can, He proceeded
despite the rebellion of man.

Could it be, for our God, that the thought made Him glad, to have
many more sons like the Son that He had.

Taking time to achieve the perfection of man, since God lives in
eternity, there's much "time" to plan.

Our Almighty God has revealed in His word, that from Gog and
Magog, much more will be heard.

They join Israel's foes, will their schemes never cease, to give them
nuclear, and say it's
for peace.

As they plot with their friends, to gather great spoil, from the Land
of God's Glory,
could it be oil?

For the search is now on under Israel's land, and the search seems to show, great reserves are at hand.

Now impelled by the hook that God put in his mouth, his greed drives him to conquer that land to the south.

In mechanized hordes like a cloud on the land, on the mountains of Israel, band after band.

Then just when they feel that they're winning the war, God will rise up in rage, fire and brimstone to pour.

In the darkness and pain each will turn on his brother, in frustrated agony, slaying each other.

And 'though other events will yet be to come, God has purposed that permanent peace will be won.

As the New Jerusalem descends from the clouds, and all men on the earth will gather in crowds.

To visit Jerusalem once every year, to worship our Savior, His blessing to hear.

And men will no longer make weapons to kill, and children are playing with asps on a hill.

And the leopard will lie with the baby goat, no longer desiring to tear out its throat.

And the lion eats straw at the oxen's feet, and wolves lie with lambs, they no longer eat meat.

For all death has been banished, rebellion is past, the suffering of mankind is over at last.

There's no more weeping or pain in the land, for sin has been banished by God's command.

And with every man's heart now wide open to pray, all pretence is erased, inner walls melt away.

Now all men will know, even as they are known, thus no longer can seeds of deception be sown.

Sly Satan, deceiving the nations he led, is now no longer free, his deception to spread.

By God's Angel he's bound with a very strong chain, then cast into hell, it's his turn to feel pain.

Now all evil and sin from the earth has been quit, for the father of sin has been cast in the pit.

And he'll never come out for a thousand years, men's hearts now delivered from all of their fears.

As the Peace of our God now on earth is ordained, men are loving each other with friendship unfeigned.

No policemen are needed, all jails have been closed, to addictions we'll never again be exposed.

Men's love for their wives will be certain and sure, as Christ's Love for the Church, perfect and pure.

From the hearts of the fathers the children are blest, each child is secure, never knowing unrest.

Men with silver and gold will abundantly share, to accumulate wealth, they will no longer care.

All the hospitals closed for disease is repealed. By the leaves of God's trees, all the nations are healed.

And here on the earth, Jesus Glory will shine, as men drink from the fountain of life for all time.

No sun or no moon will be needed for light, the Radiance of God has banished the night.

From that Glorious City with streets made of gold, He will rule man with Love, as the Bible foretold.

Walls sparkle reflects precious gems all arrayed. Twelve gates all around, of whole pearls they are made.

Why at each gate an angel, I'm not really sure, Perhaps they're on guard to keep out the impure.

And foundations twelve under girding the walls, for Apostles they're named, so no danger of falls.

We know from the Bible…you've read it, I trust. When it say's judgment's coming, then coming it must.

This message you've studied on each attached page, comes from Scripture that causes the heathen to rage.

If you'll just read the Bible and open your heart, to invite Jesus in, He will never depart.

So the choice is quite clear, God has made it that way, but the time is so short, you must choose Him today!

If now you delay, then your choice has been made. To give you this choice, with His Blood He has paid!

WAKE UP!!! YOU'RE ASLEEP!!! In this world you are lost! Choose Jesus and enter without any cost.

If you blindly continue your worldly way, God will know that hell is your choice today.

!!!!STOP!!!!
!!!CHOOSE LIFE!!!
!!!CHOOSE JESUS!!!

EVEN SO, COME LORD JESUS!

THE FREEDOM OF MY SPIRIT

By Doris Kelemen in collaboration with *Bob McCluskey July, 2008*

God created me a mortal, then my life on earth began,
Just a tiny little baby, but inside, a spirit man.
My spirit man was tested, as my flesh began to grow,
Striving started early, many battles I would know.

Battles small in the beginning, as my anger I would vent,
Loomed larger still, as against my will, to school I daily went.
My inner man was innocent, but the world looked pretty wild,
The age of innocence was past, for this frightened child.

The skills I had to learn in school, preparing me for life,
Left my spirit lacking, in the skills to be a wife.
But I graduated out of school, went looking for a job,
Submitted to the daily grind, my freedom it would rob.

My spirit had been free to fly, soaring like a bird,
I thought, is this the life I chose, I know my spirit heard.
And mourned to hear me crying, I thought I chose the best,
But now we cry together, chained together to this desk.

I knew down deep within my heart, I had to make a change,
If I prayed hard, then maybe God, a husband would arrange.
I entered into marriage, thinking love would conquer all,
And for a while, my inner man, started standing tall.

After many years of marriage, now the kids have all left home,
My spirit man was weary, as I battled on alone.
By a different kind of spirit, my husband was enslaved,
And after many battles, our home could not be saved.

The kids were fine, I'd done my job, my husband passed away,
My spirit man was joyful, I no longer had to stay.
So now as time is passing, a new life I would build,
My spirit man now came alive, I thought that he'd been killed.

Some time went by, and then one day, I met another man,
Our spirits joined so naturally, it seemed to be by plan.
We got on so well together, my spirit was content,
Life now had much more meaning, it all seemed heaven sent.

Then bye and bye, the book of life, turned another page,
The body of the one I love, began suddenly to age.
As illness had it's deadly way, his spirit wavered not,
We fought it off together, and a little time was bought.

But in God's dispensation, now the final end is known,
His spirit man departed, back to heaven, to his home.
To join with all the others, in that heavenly throng,
To eternal joy and happiness, to join in heavens song.

Now that I'm alone again, though his spirit's missed by mine,
I'm quite content to carry on, I'll join him in God's time.
For Jesus is the arbiter, of where we go and when,
With Jesus living in my heart, I'll be with him again.

SIGNS OF THE TIMES

Bob McCluskey...December, 2008

Put your nose to the wind, what can you sense,
is a smell of change in the air.
Many factors are changing in too many ways,
are we falling asleep in our chair?

Corruption's exploding in offices high,
when the choice is extended, they go for the lie.
Our leaders so devious, on each other spy,
competing like wolves for a piece of the pie.

We search the horizon for men morally strong...
there are few to be seen, whatever is wrong.
Our elections devolve into cutthroat affairs,
reputations are ruined and nobody cares.

In affairs international, evil placate,
then when going gets tough, they cave in, abdicate.
They bend over backwards, politically correct,
to protect themselves, is the choice they select.

We're exhorted by Jesus, for rulers to pray,
are we guilty of doing it, "maybe some day."
We know the end times are approaching fast,
a time when these evils will finally be past.

Occupy till I come, as good servants we're told,
Jesus wants everyone to come into the fold.
Self interest controls decisions men make,
they first want to know, how much cash will it take.

In the world we have foes, our weakness they prod,
with anger and hate, to obey their God.
Over decades they've followed a devious plan,
immigrate, separate, destroy when they can.

The priests in their temples, here in our land,
preach a gospel of conquest, and follow a plan,
Scorning our freedoms, fill their children with hate,
increase their numbers, but not integrate.

Homosexual agenda has slowly gained power,
using legal assault on our ivory tower,
With small victories daily, put down dissent,
with their gay agenda, they're never content.

Abortion mills in our land are still grinding out death,
millions of babies will never have breath.
People's lives filled with sports, entertainment and sin,
their search for God, will it ever begin.

The situation now, seems beyond our control,
but our apathy to prayer will exact a high toll,

As I write this, I see, that I'm chiefly at fault,
I've not travailed in prayer, as I know that I aught.

Please forgive me, Oh God, I've forgotten your love,
poured out on all men, from heaven above,
Your word makes it clear, to save them you came;
their Salvation is found in no other name.

So my purpose to pray, Oh God I renew,
they will never be saved, if they don't come to You.
We must all do the same, just pray in His Name,
God's Spirit will light, in their hearts, a flame.

In fact I've been told, God's already at work;
it seems praying for them, other men did not shirk.
For God's now moving across their land,
taking scales from their eyes; then for Jesus they stand.

THE SERMON ON THE MOUNT

God's instruction for happiness and fulfillment in this life
Bob McCluskey...July, 2008

Mat. 5:1,2
Our Lord climbed a mountain, and sat down to speak,
on a day perhaps like today.
His disciples came with Him, high up to the peak,
this helped keep the crowd at bay.

Our Lord was preparing, twelve men for the day,
He'd return to heaven above.
So He taught them how to establish the way,
for God's Kingdom, on earth, with Love.

V:3
Jesus taught that the poor in spirit He'd bless,
and they hung on His every word.
The Holy Spirit ministering gave them rest,
and to understand all they heard.

We cannot come to God, with an attitude sure,
but in poverty of spirit, seek the Lord.
We're blessed when our goal is His Heart so Pure,
then His Kingdom is our reward.

V:4

Next, His blessing's proclaimed on those who mourn,
at first glance it does seem strange.
Like someone who has to feel forlorn,
when a funeral they must arrange.

But God blesses the heart that mourns for sin,
the condition of all mankind.
Without Jesus, this battle they'll never win...
to the author of sin, they're blind.

V:5

He continued to teach how they'd be blessed,
when the true way to heaven they'd seek.
The one who does exploits, I would have guessed...
Jesus taught it's the one who's meek.

Did He mean one who cowers and fears to speak,
or one who would shiver and faint.
Not so, He describes one who's strong, not weak,
with his strength under God's restraint.

V:6

Now, verse six uses words that are very strong,
if we hunger and thirst, we're alive.
With all of our strength we struggle and long,
for what's needed to help us survive.

Jesus says this intensity He will bless, if,
for righteousness we're on fire.
He says we'll be filled, and I would assess,
filled with Jesus, our heart's desire.

V:7

Mercy's the theme Jesus taught upon here,
and this principle God holds high.
Once we've tasted the Salvation of God so dear,
we understand clearly why.

So, once God, from my debt, has made me free,
but my debtor I'll not forgive.
Mathew 18:35, proclaims this decree,
with the torturers I will live.

V:8

In this verse. Jesus blesses the pure in heart,
exactly what does He mean.
We talk a good game, but inside we depart,
from Truth…outward Godly seem.

Since God searches the heart by the Holy Ghost,
we're only fooling ourselves.
On the day we die, expecting God's Host…
will we end up where Satan dwells.

V:9

God's blessing falls on the peacemakers,
who relationships repair.
They'll always be known as the sons of God,
because they really care.

They're willing to enter the battlefield,
between two warring souls.
They get to the root, with the weapon of truth,
restorations always their goal.

V:10, 11, 12

Persecution is sometimes the peacemaker's lot,
when righteousness is his goal.
When exposed by truth, man feels he's been caught,
rebellion erupts in his soul.

Denying the truth, and seeking escape,
on the peacemaker he might turn.
Blind anger can cause him excuses to make,
to Jesus we pray he'll return.

But if this same sinner, will humble his heart,
and the other, seek to prefer.
Gods Spirit will show him the other's part...
from demanding his rights, he'll defer.

This infusion of mercy will restore the sight,
of the one who would not reconcile.
Both their eyes will be open to see the light,
and they'll both go the extra mile

YESTERDAY

September, 2008

As I lose my sense of humour,
They all tell me that they'd sooner,
Talk to someone who is younger,
Like yourself.
They all say that I diminish,
As I'm coming to the finish,
That I'm morphing into something,
Like an Elf.

But they're going to regret it,
I'm not going to forget it.
Though I find my memory slipping,
Just of late.
I used to be quite strapping,
And at running…overlapping,
I forget now why I'm running,
Which I hate.

I was always well proportioned,
Now my pants need to be shortened,
'cause my height's reduced.
It's caused by gravity.
I was puffing when I knelt,
So I bought a stretchy belt,

But it's not 'cause I'm expanding,
No sir-ree.

I'm just kidding 'bout my humour.
You all know that I'd much sooner,
Bring a smile upon your face,
And see you laugh.
So now I'm going to end it,
Speak the truth, try not to bend it,
Just imagine we're all young,
Like in the past.

REPENTANT SINNER

June, 2008

Oh God, please forgive me, I've been such a wilful fool,
I know I'm now a candidate, to receive the golden rule.
It say's "Do unto others, as you'd have them do to you",
But the justice there's more than I can bear, what can this fool do.

My self loathing made me hate my sin, as deep repentance grew,
Within my heart, I just gave up, now nothing could renew.
But that's what God was waiting for, to give me a brand new start,
He replaced my ugly, blackened one, with a pure, white heart.

With imagination I can see, God's Golden Chest revealed,
And within I see pure golden gifts, in His Chest that's now unsealed.
I see one called "Repentance", a shiny one, and free,
There's one that's called "Eternal Life" Oh boy, that one's for me.

Many other lovely gifts I see, it's full right to the brim.
Then God just empties out His Chest, on us, Gifts come from Him.
But God's Love is so abundant, the chest fills up right away.
Then He'll go on blessing mankind…freely, every day.

So, I know that I've wrecked havoc, brought distress into my home,
And now, sin's earthly consequence, caused me to live alone.
I love my wife and children, since my life is now on track,
My fervent prayer is that over time, somehow they'll take me back.

I know that God's forgiven me, and man, it sure feels good,
The slate's wiped clean, like it's never been, as the Bible says He
would.
But no matter how this all plays out, the die for me is cast,
I'll live for God, just do my job, till the day I breath my last.

We must all forgive each other, it's the only way, I'm told,
Imagine if we didn't, and we tread those streets of gold.
Then look, here comes another soul, who on earth we'd not abide,
And now we're meeting face to face…quick, where can I hide.

That is a little silly, but it helps to make the point,
That Jesus, as He hung that day, His bones all out of joint.
High on that cross, He paid the price, for my sin…your's as well,
So we must forgive, if we hope to live, in Heaven, not in Hell.

PRECIOUS LORD

June, 2008

Let me lean upon Your breast, Precious Lord.
Just like John, I'll be blessed, Precious Lord.
For that's the sweetest thing that I can do.
The safest place for me, is next, to you.

My Saviour…
When there are grey skies, I won't mind the grey skies,
I'll still have You, Precious Lord.
Friends may forsake me, let them all forsake me,
You'll still be true, Precious Lord.

You came from Heaven, and I know your worth,
You brought down Heaven, to me, right here on earth.

God sent You…
When I'm old and grey, Lord,
I'll never fall away, Lord.
I love You so, Precious Lord.

WHEN WE TRADED OUR HORSE FOR A CAR

February, 2008

When we traded our horse for a car,
I had visions of traveling far.
With a fervent hope, not to go up in smoke,
and become the first shooting star.

I could not feel, for this automobile,
the love that I felt for my horse.
It was cold and hard, just sat in the yard,
Indifferent to my remorse.

But I carefully entered my seat,
with bonnet on head and boots on my feet.
For I had no idea what adventures I'd meet,
as I nodded and waved all the people to greet,
who had gathered to see me depart.

In the ignition inserting the key,
fighting the impulse to flee.
For I knew all too well what ignition meant.
For my own destruction I had no intent.
All were watching with evident glee.

So I turned the key to ignite
and the racket gave me a terrible fright
I was keenly aware as I fixed my hair,
of that tank of gas just waiting to blast
and eject me into the night.

Now I had to select a gear
as I searched in terrible fear.
For a forward gear, with that wall ahead
if I made that choice, I could end up dead.

Dressed up like a lady of class
inside this box of metal and glass
I had to go on for the die was cast.

The infernal machine went into reverse
away from the wall, prim lawns to traverse.
As I frantically searched for a gear
going backwards does nothing to calm ones fear!

The rad belched steam and the gears did scream
as I frantically forced them to mesh.
The car bucked and jumped as the pedals I pumped.
With my hat on the side and my coat open wide
I was no longer looking too fresh.

But I randomly made another selection
and started to go in the right direction.
As the people began to applaud, I discreetly gave them a nod.
They think I'm alright as I race out of sight
but I'm fervently praying to God.

Now sometime I'll have to stop.
On my horse I'd use the riding crop.
But this automobile, the crop cannot feel
as it bounces with rattle and pop.

I'll try to recall the salesman's advice
as he talked down his nose to this customers wife
he described a peddle to save my life.
I CAN'T FIND IT!!

So to come to the end of this tale
Into that wall I could easily sail.
That would end my problem at once.
Then my husband would think that the brakes did fail.
and I'm not a dunce.

Maybe he'll get me another horse!

OH GOD, NO HOPE

May 2008

My friend, I hope you'll listen to, these warning words we tell
They're told with Love, from God above, to keep you out of hell
When someone talks of Jesus, do you think they've been deceived
Do you feel an anger in your heart, at this arrogance perceived

"To say that Jesus is the way, my freedom you would steal
We can't be wrong, my restless throng, who say God isn't real
How dare you tell me how to live, this life that's mine alone
How dare you force your views on me, to make of me a clone"

I understand just how you feel, I lived there many years
I'd guard my independence…you'd never know my fears
I held the same beliefs as you, that no one could impose
Their will or faith to change my life, I counted them as foes

I know you see a Christian life as boring…not too real
But just the opposite is true, a joyful change you'll feel
When Christ comes in, the sin you loved, no longer's any fun
Now sun's so bright, the grass so green, your heart loves everyone

You'll never know the joy that comes from just one little touch
God loves me and loves you too, He loves us very much
If you will overcome your mind and let your heart hold sway
God's waiting just to hear you say, "come in and have Your way"

This sweet and loving picture's of the blessing that's in store
For you the day you choose God's way, but wait, there's something
more
If you reject the Love of Christ, another fate awaits
To die in sin, let's Satan win, when life at last abates

Then you're carried down the halls of hell, a demon on each side
Escorting you with screaming hordes through gates that open wide
Like a gaping, hungry, fetid mouth, and the traffic's all one way
Your defiant words while still on earth, they hauntingly replay

You'll cry, "NO, NO, I NOW BELIEVE...I KNOW THAT IT'S
ALL TRUE
OH GOD, PLEASE GET ME OUT OF HERE, THEN I WILL
WORSHIP YOU"
If only we could pray you out, or somehow set you free
But sin can't stand before our Lord, there's nowhere else to flee.

While still on earth, the precious Blood of Jesus Christ our Lord
Was held out as a gift to you, at a price you could afford
In fact, there wasn't any charge, this gift from God was free
To cleanse your sin and keep you from the terror you now see

Oh friend, if you would only try, to see that sin is Satan's lie
This fight with God he tries to win, by keeping you enslaved in sin
Deception is his stock in trade, if you stay blind, he's got it made

That emptiness that's deep inside, cannot be filled, you cannot hide

So what's ahead? Some light? Some hope? Satan thinks you're just
a dope
Don't let him lead you by the nose, since he's the author of your
woes
Why run this race until you die, you can't be saved unless you try
Jesus stands, arms open wide, to save you, just forget your pride

I took that step at forty nine, thank God, He saved me just in time
And what a transformation came, past thirty years it's stayed the
same
Relationships were all restored, got back my wife, who I adored
The whole world turned from dark to light, I love Him now with all
my might

I know my words have been quite strong, but look at what's at stake
God weeps and wants to keep you from, this terrible mistake
Just make the choice and pray to God, I'll even help you start
"Oh God come in and cleanse my sin"…but mean it from your heart

CREATION

June 2008

How gloriously God has showered, on the world that we can see,
billions of trillions of breathtakingly, pristinely created blossoms.
When we closely scan the fragile beauty of one flowery jewel just to
examine it's symmetry, color and velvety feel, we then realize
how God's beauty is lavished on us with such abandonment.
This unimaginable variety of beauty is evidence of intentional
design.
The practical design needs, could just as easily have been
accomplished
with mundane unattractive, aesthetically ugly lumps on the ends of
stems.

And, we are blessed to admire just a few, but most bloom unseen,
anonymously decorating the air around them with a delicate
perfume.
Many are trodden underfoot. Many more are perhaps carelessly
destroyed by wildlife or storm, indifferent to their loveliness;
or to finally wilt and die. Such profusion is just a glimpse into
God's giving heart. The reality that such creative beauty is seldom,
if ever, seen or admired by men will never restrain the heart of God
from such lavish abundance. How appropriate is this line…
"Full many a flower is born to blush unseen, and waste it's
sweetness

on the desert air". Also, God makes reference to the surpassing beauty
of a Lilly, when He states that even Solomon's splendour could not compare.

Now, why would God lavish such a profusion of unique beauty on His creation, each one splendidly complete, containing within itself a reproductive capacity ensuring its annual glory.
I believe the answer lies in God's word…
First, God loves beauty, He manifests this in the Heavenly Jerusalem.
Then, God created man in His Image and in His Likeness.
And so, since we're like God, then, we love the beauty that He Loves.
And so, God, Who is Love, in His limitless Love for us, poured out upon us, this expression of his enormous capacity to bless.

May men's hearts be opened by God's Holy Spirit, to the beauty of God's Creation. May men's hearts explode with thanksgiving to our God.

MARY, MOTHER OF JESUS

December 2008

From Heaven's Throne…Jehovah God, seeing creation's mess!
Man's indelible stain, of sin and shame, lost in hopelessness.
With the Godhead all in perfect accord,
From the radiant love of God came the word,
"THE FULLNESS OF TIME IS COME".
Foundation's now laid for redemption to spread
Over earth, a shaking, man changing, sin cleansing flow, Blood Red,
Through men's hearts, though no change as yet appeared…not
yet…not yet.

Hebrew maid of Nazareth…how did God know…how could He
know;
From amongst all the virgins in Israel, no outward show, how could
He know.
But God knew your heart, unblemished, love sure, that's where God
found…a heart so pure,
For a work to begin, an assault against sin, God looks to our
heart…to the treasure within.

Ah, sweet Hebrew maid, by her mother prepared…for life…harsh
life.
Destiny's plan, she would marry a man…be a wife…a man's wife.
Sweetly, submissively, in the midst of her day, this wonder of
wonders came,

A mighty angel of God appeared; Gabriel by name.

God's earth shaking plan was about to begin, and Mary was fearful as well.

Mary was favoured by Almighty God, Gabriel started to tell…

She would bear the Son of the Most High God, conceived by God's Holy Spirit,

Unmarried and pregnant in Israel, scorned by all who would hear it.

Where Rachel wept for her children slain, God's Son is come to heal the pain.

Touched by God could she know, within her womb, she carried the hope of all men.

Instructed by God, Joseph took her to wife, and when her time was about to begin,

They must make the journey to Bethlehem, to be taxed by Herod's decree,

Pregnant, near birth, scarce more than a child…Joseph placed them tenderly,

On a donkey, and led them o'er rocky roads, for in Bethlehem they must be.

Not met with pomp or ceremony, but met with cruel rejection,

Joseph placed his wife in this shelter rough…to cradle God's perfection;

A hot, low ceiled stable filled with animal smells and animal sounds and animal dung.

On a bed of straw, with birth pangs begun…Christ's birth begun…the time is come.

Mary clung to Joseph, and brought forth a Son;

THE PROMISED ONE!…THE PROMISED ONE!

THE SON OF GOD...GOD OF ALL GLORY...HALLELUJAH! HALLELUJAH!

To shepherds nearby in fields by night,
Herald angels appeared, a wondrous sight.
With a brilliant display of the Glory of God,
With great joy, they spread the word abroad.

And from far to the east, three wise men, it's said,
Seeking King of the Jews, by a star were led,
To the stable where Jesus lay...content.
To worship on Jesus, their treasures spent.

And now God's plan...the salvation of man, was begun in earnest at
last.
After thousands of years o'er this vale of tears,
Satan's constrained at last...Yes, Satan's dominion, past.

RESTORATION

February, 2008

Scouting around just the other day,
having nothing better to do.
Went into an antique shop I like,
'cause it started to rain,
I was on my bike,
Just to look for a treasure or two.

Rummaged around,
in the back of the store,
Knew where everything was,
'cause I'd been there before,
All I could see was,
tired and wore,
like the old man in charge,
whose back was sore,
Then I noticed something new.

When I say it's new,
you know what I mean.
It's new to this store,
where it's never been.
An old three drawer dresser,
that's lost it's sheen.
One leg broke,

propped up like a crutch,
by a great thick Bible,
It's not worth much.

As I stood there in thought,
saw its finish worn bare,
I knew it had lived through,
a lifetime of wear.
Now no one would want it,
No one would care.

As I allowed my thoughts,
to wander awhile.
I imagined a woman's loving smile,
years ago as she polished,
to make it look smart,
and cherished this dresser,
with all her heart.

Then into the store,
walked another man,
a carpenter by trade.
Now this dresser's,
just what I'm looking for,
I can see it's been finely made.

Although it's been beaten,
And broken by man,

and this Bible helps it to stand.
I'll take it home,
and give it new life.
You'll never know,
that it's been through strife.
I'll make it like new,
both inside and out,
just like it's maker planned.

So I said goodbye,
and went on my way,
with my mind in reverie.
Something about,
that carpenter man,
made me think of,
The Man from Galilee.

Who finds us beaten,
and broken by life,
and will lovingly restore,
The Joy of the Lord,
we had in our youth,
as He props us up,
with His Bible Truth,
Like that dresser,
I saw in the store.

Thank You Jesus.

KING DAVID'S EARLY YEARS

September, 2008

1Sa 16:13 Jesse, the father of David, we read, had seven more sons
as well,
But David, the youngest, was chosen by God, the giant Goliath to
fell.

After Samuel imparted Gods Spirit and Power, David went back
with the sheep,
1Sa 16:12 His visage was ruddy, still only a lad, his dads flock he
would safely keep.

1Sa 17:34 Why, one day, when a lion with dinner in mind took a
sheep to enjoy a feast,
David rescued the bleating sheep from his mouth, with one blow
dispatching the beast.

1Sa 17:36 Another day, a bear entered the flock, in search of an easy
meal,
After David struck him one fatal blow, he'd nevermore hungry feel.

And so time moved along, as it usually does, and his brothers went
off to war,
1Sa 17:1 The Philistines attacked, Israel to destroy, they'd made this
attempt before.

With the war at a standstill, David was sent, to his brothers with food from Dad,
1Sa 17:17 His brothers were angry he'd left the sheep, for this danger…he's only a lad.

1Sa 17:24 There he saw Israel in disarray, when the Philistine giant came out,
He defiantly challenged their men to fight, but they ran when they heard him shout.

1Sa 17:25 To the one who would kill this Goliath from Gath, the king would give a reward,
But no man stepped forth to claim that prize; they all feared his enormous sword.

1Sa 17:45,46 Indignation rose up in David's heart, by the Spirit of God he was led,
"This uncircumcised Philistine's signed his doom; I'm going to have his head".

Without armor or sword, he crossed the ravine, with five smooth stones from the creek,
1Sa 17:45,46 "This day the Lord will give me your head, cursing God you'll nevermore speak".

I can hear the shouts from his brothers and friends, "come back, he's too big and strong",

Calling things that be not, as though they were, David ran at the Philistine throng.

He was filled with the Spirit of God and Power, as he aimed at a spot on his head,
1Sa 17:49 With the unerring power of God he swung, and that stone struck Goliath dead.

With the giants own sword, David cut off his head, and stood there holding it high,
1Sa 17:51 The Philistines turned on their heel and fled, when they saw their hero die.

1Sa 17:52 The Israelites roared a victory shout, and chased them to Ekron's gate,
All along Shaaraim Road, they cut them down, they all suffered Goliaths fate.

When King Saul heard, about what had occurred, at the valley of Elah that day,
1Sa 17:57 He sent for the hero who saved Israel, 'cause he had a reward to pay.

That's when David met Jonathan, King Saul's son, fast friends they soon became,
1Sa 18:1 David went in the army and rose through the ranks, everyone honored his name.

1Sa 18:5 A national hero he'd now become, all the women would dance and proclaim,
1Sa 18:8 "David's killed ten times as many as Saul", Saul's jealousy could not contain.

1Sa 18:10,11 An evil spirit from God then came, very forcefully on King Saul,
David's heart was pure; Saul's javelin missed pinning David right to the wall.

David knew he must leave, he'd be killed for sure, Saul plotted to take his life,
1Sa 19:11,12 Michal helped him make his escape; Saul's heart with evil was rife.

1Sa 19:18 Where he would end up, he didn't know, he'd move about day by day,
There was mortal danger to him and his wife, if in one place they would stay.

David fled to the desert, with four hundred men, malcontents, rebels and strays,
1Sa 22:2 How was he able to honor the Lord, while controlling their rebel ways.

Even asking, I know that God strengthened his hand, disobedience he'd not brook,
He would have been strong in righteousness and to God for direction look.

1Sa 22:1 So David's no longer a bit of a lad, he's grown into a godly man,
Now fleeing from Saul's demonic rage, his years in the desert began.

1Sa 22:19 One of the sons of the men of Nob, a town of Godly Priests,
Reported to David the slaughter of all, from the highest, down to the least.

1Sa 22:20 Abiathar, the son of Ahimelech, was the only one to survive,
the demonic rage of Saul who left, not a man, woman or child alive.

He slaughtered them all for not letting him know, where David was going to hide,
1Sa 22:17&23 Abiathar became one of David's men, from now on, with David he'd ride.

David's men now numbered six hundred strong, when they heard of Keileh's plight,
1Sa 23:1 The Philistine's marshalled against this town, to attack it with all their might.

1Sa 23:2 David asked of God; should he go to war, to deliver this town from their bands,
God said yes go against them and slay them now, I'll deliver them into your hands.

1Sa 23:5-7 Many Philistines fell by David's swords, the slaughter
was very great,
But now Saul was coming to trap him there, for Keilah had walls
and a gate.

1Sa 23:12 David asked the Lord, if the men of the town, would
deliver him up to Saul,
God said that they would...David knew that he should...flee from
the city's wall.

1Sa 23:19 Once more on the run, to the wilderness flee, to Ziph in
the wilderness wood,
But the Ziphites betrayed his presence to Saul, David probably knew
they would.

1Sa 23:24 So again he must flee, and I'm sure you'll agree, living
had to be pretty thin,
With six hundred men to water and feed, prospects would look quite
grim.

On the run again, how could he sustain, except for God's provident
hand,
1Sa 24:1 He fled to En-gedi to hide in a cave, with all of his rag-tag
band.

Then wonder of wonders, who's this coming in, back lit in the
entrance light,

1Sa 24:3 None other than Saul, to relieve himself; to kill him, the
men had a right.

Or so they believed, David would not agree, God's anointed they
must not touch,
1Sa 24:5,7 Instead David cut off, a small piece of cloth, from Saul's
robe, it wasn't much.

1Sa 24:8 After Saul left, a small distance away, David called; with
obeisance bowed,
Saul turned around; saw the cloth in his hand, maybe checking his
robe, wept aloud.

1Sa 24:11 "I crept up behind you and severed your coat, and you
never knew I was there,
I could just as easily have severed your throat, but I never touched
even a hair".

1Sa 24:16-22 They made peace from a distance, David feared,
Saul's unpredictable rage,
Saul turned to go home, as he wept with shame, and to David
surrendered the stage.

1Sa 25:1 Next David led away every man, to a place called the
Wilderness of Paran,
There the wicked Nabal, his business ran, he'd give help to no one, a
foolish man.

1Sa 25:5,21 Nabal's flocks, did David protect…a reward then, he
did not expect,
But at shearing time, David sent some men, from Nabal in return,
some food to collect.

1Sa 25:10,13 Nabal poured abuse on David's men, put them to
shame for seeking food,
When David heard Nabal's answer then, he swore he'd destroy him,
for being so crude.

1Sa 25:3,18 Nabal's wife Abigail, lovely to see, a possessor of
wisdom as well, was she,
Knowing David for vengeance would come to attack, loaded food on
the donkeys back.

1Sa 25:23 Her servants she hurried, David to greet, to give him this
food, his men to eat,
She followed behind, then fell on her face, in the road before David
to plead for grace.

1Sa 25:She cried out to David, to stay his hand, not kill them all, as
she knew he planned,

26 She appealed to his holy and righteous heart, from his Godly life,
he must not depart.

Her humility and beauty made David melt, he knew it was wrong,
this anger he felt,

1Sa 25:32 He knew vengeance to God belongs, as his anger abated,
knew he was wrong.

1Sa 25: Nabal, feasting and drinking at home, so drunk that his wife
just left him alone,
36,37 Next day learned what she'd done to atone, causing his heart
to become as stone.

1Sa 25:39 Ten days later Nabal expired, then his wife and
possessions, David acquired,
Abigail humbly became his wife, I'm sure she stayed with him the
rest of her life.
Though the Scripture is silent in this regard, did they celebrate in
Abigail's yard?
Was there feasting and happy rejoicing there, with plenty to eat, and
more to spare?

But after the feast, knowing Saul's wrath, they'd had to move on, so
they went to Gath,
1Sa 27:4 Now David lived on Philistine land, Saul never chased him
again, with his band.

1Sa 28:19 The Philistines now prepared for war, Saul enquired from
the witch of Endor,
Who brought Samuel back from the dead, he said that Saul would
lose his head.

And that's what happened, wounded next day, Saul fell on his
sword, himself to slay,
1Sa 31:2-4 Jonathan, David's closest friend, and his brothers also
met their end.

1Sa 31:1 All the army of Israel met defeat; many mighty men died,
their Maker to meet,
Thus, because of the terrible sins of Saul, many valiant men, in
battle would fall.

Lots more details we've had to omit, since the shortage of space
would not permit,
We'll come again, middle years to relate, and the course King
David's life would take.

KING DAVID'S MIDDLE YEARS

September, 2008

2Sa 2:1 King Saul is now dead, an era has passed, King David's
fortune turns at last.
He asked God, where his destiny lay, God said Hebron of Judah is
where you'll stay,

So he and his men, their numbers blessed, traveled to Hebron, with
all they possessed,
2 Sa 2:4 There the men of Judah, without delay, annointed him king
that very day.

2Sa 2:9 But Abner, the army commander of Saul, purposed another
plan,
The next king of Israel, this Ish-bosheth, a son of Saul, was the man.

2Sa 2:13 Ish-bosheth's men met Davids men that day at Gibeon's
Pool,
Each side provided twelve young men, to fight by the contest rule.

They broke into pairs, grabbed each others head, and thrust sword in
each others side,
2Sa 2:16 They all fell dead that day as they bled, then side rose up
against side

2Sa 2:17 That day's battle was very severe, Davids men beat the
men of Israel's king,
Ish-bosheth ruled two years, was slain in his bed; didn't seem to
accomplish a thing.

2Sa 2:25-28 Then David's men pursued Ish-bosheth's men, to the
top of a certain hill,
Where Joab and Abner made peace that day, to fight no more was
their will.

2Sa 3:1 With the house of Saul and the house of David, the war was
very long,
The house of Saul much weaker became, but the house of David
grew strong.

2Sa 3:2-5 King David had sons from six of his wives, over the next
few years,
From beautiful Abigail's son…happiness; from Adonijah and
Absalom…tears.

2Sa 3:12 After years of war between Israel and Judah, Abner worked
out a plan,
He contacted David to bring about peace, and to do it said, I am the
man.

2Sa 3:14 But David would only meet Abner, if Michal was returned
to him,
To win Saul's daughter, he slew one hundred men, and severed a lot
of skin.

2Sa 3:16 Paltiel, the man to whom she was wed, ran after her,
weeping and mad,
At Abners command, he returned to his home, but now he was
weeping and sad.

When Joab returned with his army, and learned his enemy Abner'd
been there,
2Sa 3:26 He sent messengers out to bring him back, Abner had
better beware.

2Sa 3:27 Because Abner had killed Joab's brother Asahel, Joab
demanded blood,
By a ruse he lured Abner and stabbed him, and his life poured out
like a flood.

2Sa 3:31 Heartbroken, David cried out to God, and Israel saw his
remorse,
They knew he was innocent, that God made him king, and unity
followed it's course.

2Sa 4:7 Now Ish-bosheth, Israel's king, lost courage when Abner
bled,
Then two assassins vile, stole into his room, killed him and took his
head.

2Sa 4:12 Then they took the head of Ish-bosheth, to David,
expecting a treat,
But David killed them and hung them up, and cut off their hands and
feet.

2Sa 5:3,4 So all the elders of Israel, came to Hebron and made
David king,
His age then was thirty, and forty more years of Godly service he'd
bring.

2Sa 5:6 David then purposed Jerusalem, his capital city would be,
But the Jebusites to mock him said, the lame and blind could make
him flee.

2Sa 5:8,9 His men came in by the water shaft, their victory was
complete,
He made it his home and built it up, adding to street upon street.

As David's power grew, he took more wives; more sons and
daughters he had,
2Sa 5:13,14 One of the boys was named Solomon, who'd further the
rule of his dad.

When the Philistines learned that David was king, their army massed
to attack,
2Sa 5:23 But David slaughtered their army, when God said to attack
their back.

2Sa 6:7 Next David set out for the Ark of God, to bring it to
Jerusalem,
Uzzah touched the Ark, God struck him dead, so David lost one of
his men.

2Sa 6:9-11 The fear of God entered David's heart, and that journey
came to an end,
He placed the Ark for the next three months, with Obed-Edom, his
friend.

2Sa 6:12 During all that time, God blessed the house, of Obed-Edom
the Gittite,
And when David heard this, he came back for the Ark, and
overcame his fright.

2Sa 6:16 Every six steps the bearers took, David made a blood
sacrifice,
Before God in the city he leaped and danced, and was despised by
Michal his wife.

2Sa 6:21 David declared that before his God, he would celebrate
unrestrained,
2Sa 6:23 Michal had no child to the day she died, could her attitude
be blamed.

2Sa7:2 David's heart desire was to build God a house, that He no
longer dwell in a tent,

2Sa 7:6 With Israel always moving about, God moved with them,
wherever they went.

2Samuel, chapter 7

David told Nathan that he would build, for God a permanent home,
But God said no, that God would build, a house for David alone.
And provide for God's people a home of their own, to live forever in
peace,
And plant them there to be free from care, all enemy attacks to
cease.
Furthermore, God said, that David's own son, would build the house
for God,
And the house and kingdom of David would live, no matter where
he trod.
And God would love David's son as his own, and His love would
never cease,
And establish his kingdom forever on earth; make him rich beyond
belief.

2Samuel, chapter 8

So God blessed David with great success, as he conquered all of the
lands,
Set garrisons there, great tribute to take, after slaughtering most of
their bands.
All the Gold and Silver and precious things, did he dedicate to the
Lord,
As he emptied the treasures of every tribe, all of their hidden hoard.

2Sa, chapter 9

Then David, desiring kindness to show, enquired if any were left,
From the house of Saul for Jonathan's sake, from whom he was
bereft.
A servant named Zeba reported to him, that Jonathan's son survived,
Although lame in both feet, but hidden by friends, he managed to
stay alive.

Mephibosheth, Jonathan's son was brought, and before King David,
bowed,
For the sake of his father Jonathan, great blessings David vowed.
All of the wealth of his grandfather Saul, was returned to him that
day,
Zeba and fifteen sons were commanded, to work the land right away.
And to commit to serving Mephibosheth, and to him accountable be,
While at David's table he was to sit, as his guest continually.

Now King David's life will take a new turn, not really for the best,
The next poem reveals the terrible truth, how God put him to the
test.

KING DAVID'S LATER YEARS

September, 2008

2Sa, chapter 11

When David awoke in Jerusalem one night, on the roof he took a
stroll,

And gazing down out over the town, saw Bathsheba being washed
from a bowl.

She was very beautiful to look upon, and he ordered her sent to his
room,

She conceived a child on that evening wild, now David had signed
his doom.

Next he ordered her husband returned from the war, to sleep with
her that night,

The child would be his, but he would not obey, when he came home
from the fight.

For his brothers-in-arms slept in the fields, so his concience would
not permit,

That he sleep with his wife in the comfort of home, while out in the
fields they sit.

When that ruse did not work, David sent word, that when the battle
raged hot,

They should pull the men back…leave Uriah exposed, with an arrow
he was shot.

When Bathsheba's mourning came to an end, David took her home
for his wife,
And in due time, she bare him a son, but the Lord was not pleased
with his life.

2Sa, chapter 12

The Lord commanded Nathan the prophet, to tell David this sad tale,
So that David's anger would manifest, and justice he'd cause to
prevail.
"A rich man with many flocks of his own, took a poor mans only pet
lamb,
To make a meal for a traveling friend, who came from another land".
As God would know, David's anger would flow…he said this man
has to die,
Because he had no pity, he'll restore fourfold, or I'll know the
reason why.
Nathan said to David, Thou art the man, thus saith Israel's God,
I gave you everything you desired, yet Uria's wife you did rob.
When you brought the sword on this innocent man, and also took his
spouse,
Now the sword and evil will fall on you, it will come from within
your house.

The child of this union will sicken and die, though you intercede
from the heart,

But the Lord for you will mercy show…your life will not depart.
David mourned for the child for seven days…would not take any
bread,
On the seventh day he resumed his life, when he learned the child
was dead.

Commentary on temptation
Each man, in his heart, has an area dark, always striving for
dominance,
If we don't win this war, our defeat will be sore, we mustn't give
Satan a chance.
When the temptation comes, and come it will, if we're passive, we'll
suffer defeat,
Satan brings it disguised, as good, even wise, but then he turns up
the heat.
When the deed has been done, we don't tell anyone, and function as
if we're ok,
But our heart is sore 'cause we lost that war, and from Jesus we're
slipping away.
Satan makes us believe that we can't go to God, as he works his
deadly plan,
If we'd only just focus on why Jesus died, how He paid for the sin of
each man.
Then we would remember that all have sinned, there is mercy if
we'll repent,
Then the Blood of Jesus will wash us clean, that's God's greatest
gift, Heaven sent.

To repent was a lesson that David learned, when the spirit of lust
prevailed,
But in David's life as a consequence, a tragic price was entailed.

2Sa 13:1,2 Now Amnon, one of David's sons, by a spirit of lust was
attacked,
For Tamar, the sister of Absolom, his heart with passion was
wracked.

2Sa 13:5,17 He plotted and planned to get her alone, he'd lost all
common sense,
He raped her and threw her out of his house, he would pay the
consequence.

2Sa 13:20,28 Tamar now hid in Absolom's house, and Absolom
plotted revenge,
2Sa 13:23He waited two years for just the right time, for Tamar's
shame to avenge.

He commanded his servants, when Amnon was drunk, to kill him
with a knife,
2Sa 13:28 Was that spirit of lust now on David's son, and scheming
to take his life.

2Sa 13:37 Then Absolom fled…King David was sad…because
Amnon had lost his life,
Was this Nathan's prophecy coming to pass, was this the beginning
of strife.

2Sa 14:28 Absolom fled, but was allowed to come back, in
Jerusalem to live,
2Sa 14:33 But after two years, to come into his house, did David
permission give.

2Sa 15:1 Now that Absalom found himself safely home, he put a
great plan into place,
In his heart he was scheming for David's throne, and starting to
show his face.

2Sa 15:6 Building upon his charisma bold, he set out to steal the
heart,
Of every man in Israel…he was wily, and handsome, and smart.

Was Nathan's prophecy again coming to pass, was this the extension
of strife,
Was another of David's favourite sons, going to lose his life.

2Sa 15:9,10 By a ruse he got David to let him go, and in Hebron he
worked his plan,
He announced in the land, when the horn was blown, that he was
now God's man.

When David learned about what was afoot, he knew he would have
to flee,
2Sa 15:28 To save the city from the sword, in the wilderness he
would be.

All the Levites came, with the Ark of God, But David would not
allow,

2Sa 15:25 Return the Ark to Jerusalem, it cannot stay with me now.

2Sa 15:25,26 If God looks on me with favour, I will see the Ark
again,

But if God no longer delights in me, I have no right to complain.

2Sa 16:22 Then Absalom made a public display, his dominance now
to tell,

He lay with David's ten concubines, in the sight of all Israel.

2Sa 17:24 Next he set out with his men of war, to hunt David down
in the land,

His passion for power drove him, 'gainst his father to lift his hand.

2Sa 18:7 But David's men slew of Absalom's men, twenty thousand
or more,

2Sa 18:9 And Absalom hung in the fork of a tree, his reward for
going to war.

2Sa 20:3 Then David returned to Jerusalem and re-established his
reign,

He would fight more wars with victory, and as king he would
remain.

In 2Sa 22 and chapter 23 as well, King David gave praises to God,
And recounted the works of God in his life, his loving Lord to laud.

And recounted the names of the mighty men, and the exploits of
them all,
Who followed God under David's command, who saw their enemies
fall.

2Sa 24:1 And then came a day when the anger of God, was kindled
against Israel,
He moved David to visit all the tribes, and count their numbers as
well.

2Sa When the deed was done, to count every one, David's heart was
struck with fear,
24:10 David prayed for forgiveness, God said no, from three choices
he must choose.
A seven year famine, or three months defeat, or three days plague on
the land,
2Sa 24:15 At David's choice, a terrible plague killed seventy
thousand, to a man.

1Ki 1:1 Now the time was come, as to all it must, that King David
was growing old,
Though they covered him well, he just could not seem, to get away
from the cold.

His servants came up with a grand idea, a young woman to keep him
warm
1Ki 1:3 They found Abishag, a Shunammite, his bedroom suite to
adorn.5,6 Now Absalom's mother bore another son, one Adonijah
by name,
As King David failed, he saw his chance, to bring himself great
fame.

He had many sheep and oxen prepared, and invited leaders to the
feast,
1Ki 1:9,10 And declared himself King of Israel, from the highest to
the least.

1Ki 1:33 But when David was told, he moved to install, son
Solomon as king over all,
Had him ride on David's personal mule, and sit on his throne,
Adonijah looked the fool.

Was Nathan's prophecy again coming to pass, a further extension of
strife,
Was another of David's favourite sons, going to lose his life.

1Ki 1:50 He fled to the temple, by the altar take, a hold of the horns,
for safety's sake,
King Solomon said he would mercy give, and sent him home, for
now to live.

1Ki 1:52 If he show himself worthy, he'll not lose a hair,
But if wickedness shows, for his life he'll despair.

1Ki 2:1 David now came to the end of his days...he instructed
Solomon in all his ways,
Who were his friends...who were his foes...all these things now
Solomon knows.

1Ki 2:17 Then Adonijah made a fatal mistake, David's Abishag now
his wife he'd make,
1Ki 2:23 When Solomon heard of this request, his anger began to
manifest.

1Ki 2:25 Solomon swore by God above, and sent Benaiah, who
struck him dead,
David's now lost three sons he loved, their untimely deaths by that
spirit led.

So this is the end of King David's tale, and the Godly life he led,
'Though David's Throne would forever endure, the curse on his
house, was very sure.

REAL MEN'S CHRISTMAS BREAKFAST

December, 2008

'Twas two days before New Years…downstairs in the Church,
Our men came for breakfast, and for wisdom to search.
The tables were placed in "The Porch" in their place,
For the men who we knew would be coming…by faith.

The Chef and his helpers worked hard in their lair,
In the hope that great appetites soon would be there.
With "Q's" gleaming visage and "Rich's" big smile,
Assisted by "Rev-Kev"…beating all by a mile.

Then nigh onto Eight there arose such a clatter,
But "Q" our old veteran knew what was the matter.
Away to the stove Quentin flew like a flash,
As a herd of his friends for the chairs made a dash.

Then with all of us seated and showing restraint,
Out came great trays…the smell made us faint.
Of plump steaming sausages, bursting their skins,
And mounds of potatoes…enough to fill bins.

And then trays of buns filled with ham and with egg,
We could hold in one hand, drinking juice from a keg.
And the coffee delicious with warmth and with flavor,
To be held in both hands, it's pungence to savor.

Then after we'd eaten, and offered up thanks,
There appeared at the front, coming out of our ranks.
Our jolly St. George took his place with a bound,
And we stared in amazement, as all turned around.

His eyes, how they twinkled...his dimples, how merry.
His cheeks were like roses...his nose like a cherry.
His mouth, quite expressive, was wide with a grin.
His whole face was shining, right down to his chin.

The stump of a pen he held tight in his teeth,
And his warmth encircled his head like a wreath.
He had a broad face and a corporate belly,
That shook, when he laughed, like a bowlful of jelly.

He was friendly and open, a jolly old elf,
And he held us in awe, in spite of ourself.
But a wink of his eye and a twist of his head,
Soon gave us to know we had nothing to dread.

Then he started to teach and went straight to his work,
Filling hearts with his wisdom...for us, quite a perk.
As he taught us the way to set goals and commit,
To examine ourselves, our shortcomings admit.

And when it was finished, he sprang to his car,
To his home he would fly, the distance quite far.
But I heard him exclaim, as he drove out of sight,
Remember my teaching, and please, get it right.

JESUS STANDS AT THE DOOR

November, 2008

The hour is late, our Lord's return, I sense on every hand.
Does God really mean the things He says, are we on shifting sand?
Those stories in the Bible, where evil is addressed;
If Jesus comes, won't love prevail, won't everyone be blessed.

The Bible says He loves us all, He surely won't expel,
So many who are just like me, He'll save us all from hell.
"cause after all, with income tax, we're faithful every year;
Watch what we eat and exercise…possessions, we hold dear

We're law abiding citizens, we obey the golden rule.
I'll give that guy what he deserves…he made me look a fool.
You say I should forgive him; why? Let him apologise.
I'll find a way to make him squirm, some punishment devise.

Okay, I guess we get the point…is that me described above?
I like to think I'm different, and that everyone I love.
But bring a little pressure, like a grape that's under strain.
The grape will burst, the juice will spurt…we're covered in the stain.

And doesn't that describe our plight, when someone gives offense.
Our face turns red, at what he said, let warfare now commence.
Then the stain of sin spreads over him, and over me as well
But praise the Lord, there is a way, to silence sins death knell.

That pride that's surging up inside, we must stamp it underfoot.
Just picture Jesus on the cross, all the punishment He took,
As you're standing with him, nose to nose…see him with Jesus eyes.
If in your heart you'll pray for him, you cannot then despise.

Jesus did not die, to justify, our stinking, sinful pride;
To kill our selfish inner man, is why our Saviour died.
We sin because we're sinners, while we're living in this flesh.
As we wrestle with this wickedness; Jesus strength will bless.

So, how can we have victory, when God says all have sinned?
Many times each day, along the way, with repentance turn to Him.
Confess our sin; plead for His Blood, to wash away sin's stain.
This precious gift will keep us clean…we need never doubt again.

THANK YOU JESUS

PRECIOUS BABES

December, 2008

What scene sublime,
To underline,
God's intrusion,
Into time.

Sweet little babes,
Just newly made,
By man and wife,
But God gives life.

The cycle now,
of life begin.
Dad's so proud,
looks just like him.

And mother beams,
With cradling love.
She, with this child,
Joined God above.

Now hunger pangs,
The babe awake,
His mother's milk,
He'll greedy take.

At mothers breast,
He cuddles in.
The only sound,
Soft wimperin'.

Sweet little mouth,
A buttercup,
Designed to drink,
His dinner up.

Sweet visage tiny,
Skin like silk.
Finished all,
His mother's milk.

Now eyelids close,
Mom's lullaby,
To sleep before,

NEXT HUNGER CRY!!!

IT'S TIME TO BUILD GOD'S HOUSE 2

December, 2008

Poem Verse 1

Hag 1:2 This is what the LORD Almighty says: "These people say,"The time has not yet come for the LORD's house to be built.'"

Verse 2

Hag 1:3 Then the word of the LORD came through the prophet Haggai:

Hag 1:4 "Is it a time for you yourselves to be living in your paneled houses, while this house remains a ruin?"

Hag 1:5 Now this is what the LORD Almighty says: "Give careful thought to your ways.

Verse 3

Hag 1:6 You have planted much, but have harvested little. You eat, but never have enough. You drink, but never have your fill. You put on clothes, but are not warm. You earn wages, only to put them in a purse with holes in it."

Hag 1:7 This is what the LORD Almighty says: "Give careful thought to your ways.

Verse 4

Hag 1:8 Go up into the mountains and bring down timber and build the house, so that I may take pleasure in it and be honored," says the LORD.

Verse 5

Hag 2:8 "The silver is mine and the gold is mine,' declares the LORD Almighty.

Hag 2:9 "The glory of this present house will be greater than the glory of the former house,' says the LORD Almighty. 'And in this place I will grant peace,' declares the LORD Almighty."

Verse 6

Hag 2:20 The word of the LORD came to Haggai a second time on the twenty-fourth day of the month:

Hag 2:21 "Tell Zerubbabel governor of Judah that I will shake the heavens and the earth.

Hag 2:22 I will overturn royal thrones and shatter the power of the foreign kingdoms. I will overthrow chariots and their drivers; horses and their riders will fall, each by the sword of his brother.

Verse 1

As I pondered the words of God's Prophet of old,
A strong feeling took hold, I was feeling quite bold.
As a Church we are entering into a time
Of enlarging God's House, building line upon line.

Verse 2

And I thought, we do live in large houses quite fair.
We've been blessed and we've prospered, we're comfortable there.
As we know very well, all Church room has been spent.
To harvest more souls, we must enlarge our tent.

Verse 3

We experience change, at a frightening rate.
All the prices go up, while our incomes deflate.
The world says, in its wisdom, to cut needless cost.
They see tithing to God as a wasteful loss

Verse 4

But God says if we build, then honoured He'll be.
I must try to help, that's God talking to me.
We've started already...proceeding today.
We'll keep giving and working, remember to pray.

Verse 5

God declares, the worlds wealth, all belongs to Him.
But we must do our part, before He will begin.
If we'll build it, then on it, His Glory He'll bring.
We'll have Peace, don't forget, we'll be serving our King.

Verse 6

Perilous times are upon us, God said it would be.
But the battle is Gods; He made that decree.
Look up, your redemption is drawing nigh.
Praise God, look for Jesus, He'll come in the sky.

MY VERY OWN FLU

Oct. 2008

Why do they say that I've got a cold,
when it feels like I've got a hot.
Somebody breathed on me I'm told,
now a terrible germ I've got.

I can see that ugly monster now,
just waiting his chance to infect.
I'll keep my big mouth closed somehow;
maybe that'll protect.

Oh no, I forgot about my nose;
two channels for easy access.
Wherein, I'm sure, he'll now repose,
with a pick and a shovel I guess.

With which he'll bypass my immunity,
before a defence can be set.
Then he'll create a community,
to ensure I'm more miserable yet.

Ok, here we go, now the throat gets sore,
and the phlegm starts to gather in gobs.
Sweat runs down my nose and drips on the floor,
I collapse in quivering sobs.

Then I start to complain, and no sound comes out;
what now, I've lost my voice.
So now, for help, I can't even shout;
I can hear those devils rejoice.

My ears start to get hot, I look in the glass;
good Lord, they're vermillion red.
I started to pray, but the heavens are brass;
I'm just going to hide in my bed.

One moment I'm shaking…warm I can't get,
and I pile on the covers for heat.
Next moment I'm boiling and soaking in sweat,
Kicking covers off with my feet.

I've got places to go and things to do,
but can hardly crawl out of bed.
Did this come from the land of Hong-Kong-flu;
they live upside down there, it's said.

This can't last forever, You'll soon be better,
the undertaker assured.
I'll just medicate up and put on a sweater;
thank God, my demise is deferred

If you don't see me hangin' around for awhile,
don't worry, I'm not really dead.
My carcase will soon escape this trial;
by God's grace, I'll get out of this bed.

THANKS FOR THE MEMORIES

November, 2008...on retirement from Men's Ministry leadership council

Hey thanks, for the memories;
I'd shake my sleepy head, evacuate my bed;
The Pastor's there, no breakfast fare, just coffee hot instead.
But, thank you, so much.

Hey thanks, for the memories;
Those mornings in the rain, together once again;
To plan ahead, it can't be said, our meetings were in vain.
So, thank you, so much.

How many times I remember, those decisions together we made;
From January through to December;
We did have fun, now I must run.

So thanks, for the memories;
It's time to make a change, this council rearrange;
Richard and Matt, they filled the gap, a wonderful exchange.
So, thank you, so much.

CREATION'S MYSTERIES

September, 2008

How awesome to see God's Creative selection
Each creature designed with exquisite perfection
Elephants large or fleas microscopic
So busy with life from Artic to Tropic

When my kitchen was plagued with the pesky fruit fly
I embarked on an orgy of killing to try
To wipe them all out, they all had to die
But the more I destroy, all the more multiply

Surely not resurrected, 'cause completely dissected
Their pieces I washed down the sink
Now they cannot attack, but when I turn my back
They reappear, quick as a wink

Somewhere in my house, in a well hidden lair
Must be millions of fruit flies, each half of a pair
Ecstatically active in race reproduction
Multiplying more quickly than I wreck destruction

They ebb and they flow, sometime there are lots
But from searching intently, I start to see spots
On white cupboard doors, when there's nary a fly
Persecuted I feel, I might even cry

I paused my frenetic assault…out of breath
I'm frustrated…as if life has overcome death
Though many I massacred, more would appear
Curiosity piqued…I conquered my fear

As I gazed more intently at my latest victim
Who fell for my ruse…this time I tricked'm
Then I saw, a quite perfect, clear gossamer wing
So tiny, so fragile, a beautiful thing

And of course they have two, to propel them with ease
With muscles to move them, as fast as they please
And with blood in their veins, I've seen the red stain
All they need to live life, maybe even a brain

And they have some device that detects rotting fruit
Could that possibly mean they're adorned with a snoot
And they must have a mouth, 'cause if I leave my chair
They alight on the plate, my dinner to share

As I watched him lie in my hand so still
I realized this creature could exercise will
Motivated perchance by hunger or fear
With annoying speed, out of reach he'd veer

But this time I got him, he'll not fly again
Though I couldn't help sensing a bit of his pain
This tiny perfection got what he deserves
But don't grieve, please help, they've sent in the reserves.

CONGRATULATIONS!

Folks, try as I might, I can't hide my delight, a rumour I recently heard

To say who told me, wouldn't be right, let's just say it's a little bird

Dea and Bob are about to be wed, they're going to tie the knot

Bob's the winner here, read on to see, he's going to gain a lot

Pro 31:10 A wife of noble character who can find? She is worth far more than rubies.

Pro 31:11 Her husband has full confidence in her and lacks nothing of value.

Pro 31:12 She brings him good, not harm, all the days of her life.

Pro 31:15 She gets up while it is still dark; she provides food for her family…

Pro 31:17 She sets about her work vigorously; her arms are strong for her tasks.

Pro 31:20 She opens her arms to the poor and extends her hands to the needy.

Pro 31:23 Her husband is respected at the city gate, where he takes his seat among the elders of the land.

Pro 31:25 She is clothed with strength and dignity; she can laugh at the days to come.

Pro 31:26 She speaks with wisdom, and faithful instruction is on her tongue.

Pro 31:27 She watches over the affairs of her household and does not eat the bread of idleness.
Pro 31:30 Charm is deceptive, and beauty is fleeting; but a woman who fears the LORD is to be praised.

AND SO, FRIENDS…

With a heart of love, I endorse the above, may God bless you both today

To "Prefer one another in love", God says, this is the blessed way

It's the sacrificial way to live, we get back so much more than we give

You've many more years to prove it's true, many years together to live.

June 2008

AN EVENING WITH STEVE AND SHU

Sung to the music, "Tea for Two"

Tea for two, with Steve and Shu
The evening was lovely, the time really flew
The dinner was great, and I ate every scrap on my plate, dear

The guest list for dinner, was filled out with taste
The evening was restful, with no need for haste
Conversation had spirit; I hope I gave others a chance, dear

We all had, a wonderful time, sharing together, we didn't need wine
We were blessed by the Lord, through our hostess, the Empress Shu

A LOVE TO REMEMBER

September, 2008

Remember when none of our bodies hurt
Remember…before we were older than dirt

We used to hate baths, now it's hours in the tub
What used to be muscles, have turned into flub

That great shock of hair's, now a few wispy strands
Doc says fat's from gorging, I'm sure it's from glands

Back then we would run up that hill to the top
But now, just the prospect, can cause us to flop

My wife says I'm forgetting, and saying things twice
My wife says I'm forgetting, and saying things twice
But that can't be true…now try to be nice

And at Easter that joke puts a smile on my face
I can hide my own Easter Eggs…Lord, I need Grace

Sure, I know that my memory's becoming a pain,
But each day I meet folks for the first time…again

But there's someone I know I will never forget
My children and grandchildren…each one a pet

And my friends in the Lord, they bring love all around
When love's not extended, yet with love they abound

And one thing to remember, we're all very secure
In the love of our Lord, because His Love is sure

FIRST LOVE

June, 2008

Some of you are still young, love's delights lie ahead
Your priorities now involve games, food and bed
You can jump and cavort with reckless abandon
One day though you'll care, for the part you might land on

I'm really addressing you men who are not
Quite as young as you once were, but still care a lot
Remember your first love, that first tender kiss
You meandered for days with your head soaked in bliss

C'mon guys, you remember…you almost could prance
When the love of your life would just give you a glance
Why, you'd climb every mountain, or slay every dragon
To have on your arm, this sweet lady to brag on

Now, my purpose in this is to help you remember
The days when your love was so sweet and so tender
Then refocus that thinking to Heaven above
How intensely He loves, for it says God *IS* Love

Not, has love, or gives love…much stronger you'll see
Could God possibly feel the same feelings as me
Yes, but not only that, His love's pure and complete
And much, much more intense, it's impossibly sweet.

Now, some might think I'm prone, to embellish this story
And perhaps you'd have grounds, for He won't share His Glory
But He bathed me in Love, indescribably sweet
So compellingly Lovely, I fell at His feet

Now, my words, while quite honest, cannot rank with God
This would be sacrilegious, His Glory to rob
But His sweet love's revealed…how His Great Heart does long
You can read it yourself…it's in Solomon's Song

MY JOURNEY'S END

Please don't weep for me, when I've come to the end,
    Of this journey on earth we call life.
God has blessed me so much, with family and friends,
    And a lifetime of joy with my wife.

    All of my friends, in the East and the West,
    Have been travel companions, unmatched.
    As together we've shared, in each others lives,
    And our problems together dispatched.

Each friend who has walked, by my side on this trip,
    Showered love on me through every season.
I'm only concerned, that their love I returned,
    And to hurt them, I never gave reason.

    But the greatest regret's that I lived my own life.
    I knew not, nor cared not for God.
    For the first fifty years Jesus love was rebuffed,
    While the debt that I owed Him, I'd rob.

    Our Lord is so faithful, He never gave up.
    He knew just when I'd open heart's door.
    At the potential loss, of the wife that I loved,
    In my heartbreak His Love He would pour.

These eyes that were blind, He would open at last,
As His wonderful Truth was revealed.
Then He showed me ahead, a new golden path,
Sin's death penalty, now was repealed.

So to all of my friends, who've not taken this step,
If God's Truth seems too good to be true.
Just open your heart and say, "Jesus, come in",
I'll be waiting in Heaven for you.

SEE YOU ALL IN HEAVEN...By God's Grace

Bob McCluskey
Recycled by God